The Far East –

including
Thailand, Malaysia, Bali, Singapore and Hong Kong

REG BUTLER

In Association with

THOMSON HOLIDAYS

SETTLE PRESS

Text © 1994 Reg Butler
3rd Edition 1997

First published by Settle Press
10 Boyne Terrace Mews
London W11 3LR

ISBN (Paperback) 1 872876 59 5

Printed by Villiers Publications
19 Sylvan Avenue
London N3 2LE
Maps by Mary Butler

Foreword

As Britain's leading holiday company operating to Thailand and other destinations of the Far East, Thomson are happy to be associated with Reg Butler's latest guide-book to the region.

The author has travelled annually for around two dozen years throughout Asia, and is well qualified to write about the history, culture and cuisine of these fascinating lands.

Whichever destination you have chosen for your holiday, we feel this pocket book can act as a quick reference guide to the great sightseeing potential beyond the beaches. In writing the book, the author has also worked closely with our own locally-based staff and agents who have year-round contact with holidaymakers' travel interests.

Prices are always a problem during a time of variable inflation and exchange rates. Inevitably there will be some local changes since this edition was printed. However, the prices mentioned should still give a reasonable indication of the average level of expenses to expect.

THOMSON HOLIDAYS

Contents

Chapter One

Gateways to the Orient

For the westerner on a first-time journey to the Far East, the great diversity of cultures and lifestyles makes an overwhelming impression.

In Europe we think there's a huge difference between the British, Russian, Greek and Spanish ways of life. But the range is infinitely wider in Asia. The rural patterns of Thailand and Bali have great similarities, but they're a whole world apart – centuries removed – from the high-rise urban living of Hong Kong or Singapore.

The ethnic diversity of southeast Asia is fascinating: Chinese, Thai, Malay and Indonesian, with a fair sprinkling of Indian. Each community has kept its customs and religion, but often modified after generations of intermarriage. The great Asian religions dominate everyday life: Buddhist, Hindu and Muslim. Temples, shrines and colourful festivities give rich variety to the local scene.

Ever since the first century AD, several waves of new ideas have swept through southeast Asia, modifying its development. The lead was first taken by India. The concepts of Buddhism and Hinduism followed the Indian model, with philosophy, arts and classical dance being gradually introduced by Indian priests, scholars and merchants.

Arab traders brought Islam to Indonesia in the 13th century, and the religion spread through Malaysia two centuries later.

The Chinese contribution came from its people, who settled as artisans and traders in most of the region's major cities. In their Chinatowns they built temples and kept their strong traditions of craftsmanship, cuisine and festivities.

SOUTHEAST ASIA

| 0 | 200 | 400 |
miles

8

The colonists arrive

Chinese influence also spread into the decorative
arts. Typically the ceramic skills of Thailand came
from China in the 13th and 14th centuries.

From the 16th century the western powers arrived
– first the Portuguese, then the Dutch, British and
French. For 400 years these powers dominated the
region, with Thailand alone staying independent.

The colonial period soon brought major shifts of
population from the countryside to the new cities. In
Malaysia, Chinese immigrants swept in to settle former jungle areas. Later, Chinese and Indian minorities became part of the established structure of the
European power centres which widened the gap between rural and urban life.

Today, Singapore and Hong Kong are the economic tigers of southeast Asia, great financial and
commercial centres which are world leaders in the
technology of the millenium.

In the fast-moving world of the 90's – here today
and Hong Kong tomorrow – Asian travel has never
been easier. Bangkok, Kuala Lumpur, Singapore and
Hong Kong are the wide-open airport gateways that
bring even the most remote areas within reach of a
two-week holiday.

The tropical-paradise beaches of Phuket, Penang
or Bali are just an overnight journey from Europe,
America or Australia. They are great destinations for
honeymooners, devotees of watersports, or anyone
who just wants a week or two of relaxation.

But only a short distance from the palm-tree resorts is all the fascination of exotic sightseeing, rich
cuisine, traditional culture and craftsmanship. An
endless choice of discoveries awaits the traveller:
elephant roundups, colourful markets, festivities,
beautiful dancing, the cycle of the rice harvest.

An ideal combination is to link one or more of the
gateway cities, packed with excitement, with the
more tranquil island setting of Phuket, Penang or
Bali. There's even the possibility of combining a
southeast Asian cruise with a beach resort.

Thailand, Malaysia and Bali especially must rate
among the world's best value sunseeker destinations.
Paradise now is an affordable luxury.

Chapter Two

Planning to go

2.1 The weather to expect

Thailand has a rainfall pattern that varies according to region. The southwest monsoon brings heavy rains thoughout Thailand from June till October, but from May along the Phuket side of the peninsula.

Southern areas of Thailand, including Ko Samui in the Gulf of Thailand, also have November to January rains brought by the northeast monsoon, but are less affected by the summer monsoon. The northeast monsoon bypasses the rest of Thailand.

In northern Thailand, and south to Pethburi Province, the climate divides into three distinct seasons: dry (March – May), wet (June – October), and cool (November – February).

Temperatures reach well into the 90s F during the hottest months of March and April, and can drop to 65° F in Bangkok in December. Temperatures in Phuket and Ko Samui are more constant throughout the year, usually in the upper 80s.

Malaysia offers year-round summer, warm and sultry with midday temperatures steadily around 90° F. Evenings are cooler, and very pleasant with minimum temperatures of average 73° F.

Away from the mountain areas, Penang has much lighter rainfall than Kuala Lumpur, and is more concentrated by the southwest monsoon between May and November. Tropical downpours refresh the air, and the sky clears after an hour or two.

The weather to expect:

Max — Average maximum temperatures — °F. *Rain — Monthly rainfall in inches.*

	Jan	Feb	Mar	Apr	May	Jun	Jul	Aug	Sep	Oct	Nov	Dec	Annual rainfall
THAILAND													
Max	89	90	90	91	91	87	84	84	85	88	91	91	
Rain	.1	.0	.2	.4	.7	22.8	35.1	13.4	10.9	4.8	.8	1.5	90.7"
MALAYSIA													
Max	90	92	92	91	91	91	90	90	90	89	89	89	
Rain	6.2	7.9	10.2	11.5	8.8	5.1	3.9	6.4	8.6	9.8	10.2	7.5	94.1"
SINGAPORE													
Max	86	88	88	88	89	88	88	87	87	87	87	87	
Rain	9.4	7.5	7.9	7.5	6.9	6.9	7.2	7.7	7.3	8.9	10.0	10.2	97.4"
HONG KONG													
Max	64	63	67	75	82	85	87	87	85	81	74	68	
Rain	1.2	1.8	2.8	5.3	11.4	16.0	14.5	14.4	10.9	3.9	1.7	1.0	84.9"
BALI													
Max	87	88	87	88	87	86	85	86	86	86	90	88	
Rain	15.0	11.8	9.0	5.9	5.1	5.9	5.1	3.1	2.0	5.1	9.8	11.8	89.6"

Singapore is warm and humid year-round, with slight variations between the average daytime maximum of 88° F and minimum of 74°. There is no marked wet or dry season. Short sharp downpours provide refreshing interludes to the warm, sunny climate. Thunderstorms occur on 40% of all days. February is usually the sunniest month.

Hong Kong has a sub-tropical climate with four distinct seasons. In spring (March to May) the average temperature is around 70° F. In summer it soars into the upper 80s and the humidity is high. From late September until early December the climate is very pleasant with sunny days, temperatures around 75° F and less humidity.

Most rain falls during the summer months and typhoons can blow up between June and September. Winter in Hong Kong goes from December to March and the climate can often be quite fresh and chilly.

Bali has a deliciously warm climate throughout the year with temperatures hovering in the mid 80s F. The drier season is from mid-April to September, but even during the wet season you can expect long sunny periods interspersed with sudden tropical showers. Bali can be very humid all year round.

2.2 Visa and entry regulations

UK holidaymakers to Thailand, Malaysia, Singapore, Hong Kong and Indonesia can enter without a visa, on production of a valid passport and a confirmed onward or return ticket. In case of any change in the rules, re-check for Hong Kong before departure.

Exceptionally a visa for Thailand is required **if you plan to stay longer than 30 days**. The short-time entry cannot be extended within Thailand itself.

If you need a Thailand visa, apply to any Thai consulate - in Britain, the Royal Thai Consulate at 30 Queen's Gate, London SW7 5JE. Enclose a s.a.e; or call at 29 Queen's Gate 9.30-12.00 hrs on weekdays except on UK or Thai public holidays.

Two passport-sized photos are needed, and a fee of £8. Allow ten days to process postal applications.

The visa should be used within three months. For more information on Thai visas, phone 0891-600150 (costing 39p per minute off-peak).

2.3 What to pack and wear

Pack light shirts and dresses of the drip-dry variety. A jacket and tie is required only in top restaurants and nightclubs, and is a useful precaution against excessive air-conditioning. If you are taking a cooler-season tour to northern Thailand or to Malaysia's Cameron Highlands a sweater may be needed.

Depending on your destination and the season, pack a plastic mac or folding umbrella.

It's worth travelling out deliberately short of clothes, to give yourself a good excuse to go shopping for low-cost garments. A wide brimmed beach hat and sun glasses are recommended, and comfortable shoes or sandals for sightseeing.

Don't forget suntan lotion, toiletries and any medicines which you take regularly. The range available at your resort destination may not include your preferences.

Hotels provide basic equipment for the usual holiday sports. But dedicated tennis players, for instance, should bring their tennis racket. Watersport equipment can be hired.

2.4 Health care

There is no *obligation* to produce vaccination certificates when arriving direct from Europe or North America. But some jabs are recommended, and vaccination records should be checked.

Ask your own doctor's advice at least six weeks before departure. Some medical people lean heavily towards ultra-caution, and recommend the full works – cholera, typhoid, polio, malaria – suitable for soldiers engaged in jungle warfare. Others suggest that some jabs are not essential if you take normal care of yourself, and do not visit any outlandish areas.

For up-dated health advice contact the Hospital for Tropical Diseases Healthline on 0839 337 722. Code number is 55. A phone charge is made of 36p a minute in off-peak hours; otherwise 48p a minute.

Mosquitoes

Quite apart from the dreaded female *anopheles* mosquitoes who can cause malaria, have your defences ready against all the other varieties of biting insects. Mosquitoes and sand flies bite especially at dusk when hungry for supper. They are very partial to holidaymakers. Be frugal with perfumes and after-shaves, as these seem to attract them. Insect repellents are sold in hotel shops.

An excellent mosquito deterrent is (believe-it-or-not) Avon's 'Skin-so-soft' bath oil spray. It's highly effective. Even sand-flies will keep their distance.

For a peaceful night's sleep, keep your windows closed after dark, and have any mosquito screens in place. Leave the air conditioner switched on.

It's worth packing an electrically-operated mosquito kit, which can be remarkably effective, vapourising an insect repellent throughout the night. The kits are usually available in the airport shops when you depart from UK. Don't encourage other insects by leaving food around in your room.

Water

Mains water is chlorinated, and may cause some stomachs to protest until accustomed to the flavour, though Singapore and Hong Kong should cause zero problems. Otherwise it's best to be cautious.

Most hotels in Thailand and Bali provide reliable cold water in flasks at your bedside, and there's nothing to worry about in the drinks and ice cubes served in hotels and good restaurants.

Elsewhere, buy bottled mineral water. If buying bottled water from street vendors, check the cap to ensure it is properly sealed. Sometimes bottles are refilled with tap water and resold to unsuspecting tourists.

Stomach upsets

Most upsets are caused by unaccustomed food, very cold drinks and hot sun. If you're not accustomed to quantities of fresh fruit, go easy at first with all that tempting tropical produce. Give your stomach time

to attune itself to a deluge of pineapple juice and
fruit punches.

Choose eating-places with care and eat hot foods
while they are hot. If you have trouble with spicy
foods, ask the waiter which dishes are less spicy.

In Thailand and Indonesia, be wary about down-
market local restaurants and street food stalls, where
kitchen standards may be less than ideal.

In Singapore and Hong Kong, with their dedica-
tion to ultra-fresh food, there should be no problems,
wherever you eat.

Chapter Three

Land of the Thai smile

3.1 The charm of Thailand

If you want a two-week sample of Asia, put your money on Thailand. There's a friendliness about the country. In tourism marketing, promotions often mention the 'Thai smile'. This doesn't mean everyone goes around grinning like a Siamese cat. But the cheerful look goes with plentiful laughter.

With good rains and hot sun, food grows fast in this rice-bowl of Asia. The affluent Western visitor can feel comfortable as he strolls around, taking pictures. Everyone looks well-fed, and beggars are rare. Thais believe in *sanuk* – the art of having fun.

In a warm climate, dress is casual, needs are simple, and housing costs are minimal, with a coconut-palm thatched roof erected in 24 hours. That's an advantage over paying mortgage interest for 24 years. Something to Thai-smile about!

Thailand offers a widely contrasting choice of holiday experience. Bangkok, a steaming city of over six million inhabitants, may seem far removed from those romantic visions about life in old-time Siam: ever-smiling dancers in silken costume, glittering festivals, working elephants, and the unchanging tranquillity of the countryside.

But within an easy drive or river cruise of the capital, most of those memorable sights can come within day-trip range. They are even closer for anyone staying at the beach resorts.

To experience the charm of legendary Siam, it's worth spending a few days in the beautiful northern region of Thailand, centred on the ancient capital of Chiang Mai.

Thai diversity

Historically exposed to the widely different cultural
influences of India, Burma and China, Thailand divides geographically into three distinct regions.

The south, bordered by the Andaman Sea and the
Gulf of Thailand, is renowned for its beaches and
rich fishing, which have both overtaken rubber plantations and tin mines in economic importance.

The centre is a broad plain irrigated by the Chao
Phraya River and its tributaries. This highly fertile
region supports most of the country's population in
a peaceful farming style little changed across the
centuries.

In the north, broad valleys between high mountains are carpeted with teak forests, where logging
camps still use working elephants. The northeastern
plateau has been revealed by recent archaeological
discoveries as the home of one of the world's earliest civilisations, dating from around 3,600 BC – 600
years older than Egypt's.

About 95% of Thais are Theravada Buddhist. The
Thais call their religion 'Lanka-Vamsa Buddhism'
because the religion came originally via Sri Lanka.
Thousands of graceful Thai temples (called wats),
with their several rooms and slender spires, support
monastic communities and also act as social centres,
schools and hospitals.

Early every morning, young and elderly saffron-
robed monks wander out with their begging bowls,
to be given alms, food, incense and lotus flowers by
devout Buddhists.

Almost two-thirds of the population still rely on
agriculture for a living. Cottage industries flourish,
with products that reflect centuries of traditional
craftsmanship. Silk and cotton weaving, lacquerware,
woodcarving, basketry and jewellery carry the hall-
mark of Thai creativity.

Despite the ethnic mix of Thai, Chinese and Malay, Thailand can feature its own style in festivals
and ceremonies, architecture (houses are on stilts,
with gables), painting and splendid dance-drama. The
country offers a cultural experience that is quite different from its Asian neighbours.

Certainly there's more to Thailand than gorgeous
temples and beaches. To explore beyond your hotel
complex can be very rewarding.

3.2 Arrival and orientation

For most nationals who arrive with a valid passport and a return or onward ticket, no visa is required for visits up to 30 days. For anyone planning to stay longer, a transit visa is required – see section 2.2 of this book.

Once you have passed through immigration and collected your baggage, you'll find tour reps outside the Customs exit. Thomson's customers are greeted by a Thomson representative or a guide from their local agency, Turismo Thai.

Individual travellers can buy a taxi ticket to their hotel from a booth which gives set prices. There are efficient and low-cost bus and mini-bus services to downtown locations.

Don Muang International Airport is 15 miles north of central Bangkok. If you are staying in Pattaya – south of Bangkok – the 90-mile journey by motorway takes about 2 hours 30 minutes.

Many beach-lovers fly direct to Phuket from Britain by charter aircraft. On arrival there, Thomson clients will be met by a Thomson or agency representative and taken to their chosen hotel.

3.3 At your service

Money: The Thai unit of currency is the baht (B) divided into 100 satang (which has minimal value). Thai currency is very stable, now linked to the US dollar at around 30 baht.

Depending on the strength of sterling, you can expect up to 50 baht to £1.

Banks are open Mon-Fri 8.30-15.30 hrs, but the licensed money changers often stay open seven days a week from 8.00-20.00 hrs. Hotels generally give a lower rate of exchange.

International credit cards are welcome in Bangkok and major tourist centres. Eurocheques are accepted by the Thai Farmers Bank, but not in shops or restaurants.

Transport: Metered taxis are widely available in Bangkok, but not elsewhere. Fares are reasonable and tipping is not necessary. If your taxi has no meter, always agree a price before starting.

Typical fares in Bangkok range between 40 and 150 baht. Hotel taxis operate to fixed rates which are usually more expensive, though the drivers are more likely to speak some English.

'Tuk-tuks' (also known as *samlors*) are motorised three-wheeler taxis that sound like mobile chain-saws at full speed. They are cheap – roughly half the price of regular taxis – and amusing to ride for short distances. However, few drivers speak English, so you need to have your destination written out in Thai. Pedal samlors (bicycle rickshaws) are available in many places.

Buses are very crowded and cheap, around 5 baht a journey, but destinations are displayed only in Thai.

In Pattaya and Phuket, taxi vans with open sides are the best way to travel around. They will usually take you to your destination for a minimum rate of 25 baht.

If you want to hire a car – *not* recommended for Bangkok unless you have nerves of steel – you will need an international driving licence. Traffic is supposed to keep to the left. Motorbike hire comes without any protective gear, and is the biggest single source of hospital casualties in Phuket.

3.4 Thai cuisine, and eating out

The Thais take pride in their cuisine, which offers excellent value for money. Dining out is a delight, especially if you like pungent and spicy dishes enlivened with garlic and chillies.

Thai food is normally prepared with fresh ingredients and includes fish, poultry, pork and some beef, with rice as the foundation. When you try the spicy dishes, take a tip from the Thais and eat plenty of steamed rice to cool you down.

If you want to follow Thai table etiquette, eat food with a spoon in the right hand, using a fork only to push food onto the spoon, but not into the mouth. Chopsticks are used for noodles. Sticky rice, popular in the north, is rolled into a ball and eaten with right hand only – *never* the left hand.

Food specialities

Just about everything in Thai cuisine is different
from your own home cooking.

Among the hundreds of dishes to investigate are a
seafood curry with vegetables and coconut milk,
served in a 'basket' of banana leaves (don't eat the
leaves!); prawn soup seasoned with lime juice and
red pepper; 'paw pia tod' – a feather-light pancake
enclosing sweet and sour crabmeat, bean sprouts and
pork; and 'gai hor bei toey' – morsels of chicken
fried with sesame oil, soya and oyster sauce.

Different Thai regions have distinctive cuisines,
but they all share the hot-spice characteristic. A typical curry is made with peppers, fresh herbs and
shrimp paste, blended with sweet coconut milk and
served with rice.

If it feels as though your tongue has blistered, and
the enamel has been scaled off your teeth, eat more
rice, quickly. But restaurants that cater for western
visitors usually go easy with the peppers and chillies,
and add more coconut milk.

Many of the dishes have no easy translation. In
the more unpretentious restaurants there's often good
fun from reading menus which make valiant attempts
to explain Thai dishes in tasty English.

If all these delights do not appeal, western food is
widely available in hotels, and there are numerous
fast-food chains in the cities and resorts.

The most economical eating places are noodle
shops and night markets. Snack bars offer little plastic bags of sliced fruit; or sticky rice cooked in bamboo stalks with coconut milk; dried squid, fried
chicken, noodles; hard boiled eggs, peanuts, shred-
ded salad; and a variety of sugary sweets.

Fruit juices and beverages

In local markets, fruits are piled high – pineapple,
banana, oranges, water melons, papaya, mango and
exotic tropical fruits which may be hard to identify.
Many are converted into juices and shakes, usually
with added salt unless you stop the vendor in time.

In Thai and Chinese restaurants, weak lukewarm
tea is poured from metal teapots during the meal,
usually at no charge. An order of hot tea or filtered
coffee normally comes sugared and with condensed
milk. Instant coffee is served with packet creamer.

Among the alcoholic drinks, try Singha beer, or Kloster which costs a little more. Larger bottles are the better value. The local alcohol is the rice-based Mekong 'whisky', which is less potent than the real thing. Try it with soda water. Other brand names are Hong and Kwangthong.

Wine is extremely expensive. A bottle often costs more than the meal itself. Likewise, well known western branded drinks can be expensive if imported instead of being locally produced under licence.

3.5 Nightlife and entertainment

Bangkok and Pattaya have achieved a certain notoriety for nightlife on the wild side. The districts of Patpong in Bangkok and 'The Strip' in Pattaya are where most 'girlie bars' are located.

Phuket is likewise well endowed with what the locals call 'bar-beers' – a square open-air bar with a girl smiling from each side. Patong especially has lots of bars, restaurants, good atmosphere and street markets selling everything. Delightful!

At all the main Thai resorts, there are delicate displays of classical Thai dancing – either as a full performance with dinner, or as part of a general show that also includes the spectator sports of martial arts or Thai kick-boxing.

Many leading hotels also offer western style cocktail bars, nightclubs and discos.

Classical Thai dancing: The very expressive traditional dance-dramas of Thailand can feature 64 main attitudes, each of which has its own meaning. There are five principal styles of dance-drama, each designed originally for different levels of audience from the royal court to popular village festivals. They originate mainly from India and Sri Lanka.

The famous 'fingernail dance' comes from northern Thailand. The aim is for the richly costumed dancers to show off their long and delicate brass fingernails as a prestige symbol to prove they were noble creatures who did no manual work.

Whichever performances you attend, there are always plentiful opportunities for colour photography of masked monkey and demon figures, superbly graceful female dancers with glittering head-dress, and the musicians themselves who play flutes, gongs and xylophones. Don't forget your flashgun.

Thai boxing: This is boxing in which everything goes – hands, knees, feet and elbows. While your opponent is aiming a swift right-foot to your ear, you can get him with a quick knee to the stomach or trip him up. All is fair, Thai style.

With knees, fists and feet going simultaneously, Thai boxing demands great skill and split second timing. It's all done to the music of drums and pipes, and must be rated among the world's most agile professions.

3.6 Shopping

Shops are usually open from 10.00-20.00 hrs every day. Always bargain when buying from markets and small shops, but department stores have fixed prices. Beware of friendly touts who offer to help you shop, as their commission will hamper your chance of a realistic price.

Thailand may not offer such a wide range of high-tech bargains as Singapore or Hong Kong, but it's still a shopper's paradise. The best buys include Thai silks and cottons, silver, bronzeware, woodcarvings, ceramics and celadon (a high-fired stoneware with a greyish green or grey blue glaze). Clothing can be made to measure in 24 hours, though it's advisable to allow more time for proper fitting.

Good areas for shopping in Bangkok are the Siam Centre, Silom Road and Pratunam Market.

In Pattaya visit the local market, Na Klua, for T-shirts, leather goods and beachwear. Specialities from Phuket are pearls, niello ware (silver inlaid with a black alloy), sea-shells and just about everything else.

Genuine or fake?
The Chiang Mai area is best for celadon, silver craftsmanship and handwoven silk and cotton. Woodcarvings are everywhere: hundreds of teak bowls and rank upon rank of wooden elephants and smiling Buddhas.

For anyone seeking goods with prestigious designer labels, Bangkok is a faker's paradise. But the quality doesn't always rival that of the real thing.

Precious and semi-precious stones are not necessarily a bargain in Thailand. On show are displays of costume jewellery and gem stones – tourmaline, sapphires, topaz, tiger-eye, smoky topaz, amethyst, yellow sapphire, white zircon, garnet and rubies.

The buyer should beware. It is not a crime to sell over-priced stones to tourists who think they are getting a 'deal'. In reality few bargains exist, and you should not speculate in gem-stones unless you have virtually professional knowledge. A shop may look very established, but could still sell fakes.

If you do decide to 'invest' in valuable gem-stones, it's best to buy them pre-set or have a setting made in Thailand. You will then have an attractive piece of jewellery even if it's not as valuable as you may hope.

Following many incidents where British tourists have been defrauded, the advice from the British Embassy in Bangkok is *not* to buy expensive gems unless the shop gives a certificate of authenticity. This will improve your chance of getting a refund if you find out quickly enough that you have been sold a fake. It is illegal to sell one thing whilst describing it as another.

Sacred images of Buddha or other deities may not be exported, irrespective of value. Antiques and genuine works of art require a special export certificate which can easily take three weeks to obtain.

The Thais are currently doing their utmost to save the Asian elephant from extinction. Help the cause by refusing to buy ivory, or any shoes, wallets or handbags made of elephant hide.

3.7 Festivals and public holidays

The basic public holidays are:

Jan 1 – New Year's Day.
February full moon – Makha Bucha, a Buddhist holiday ending in candle-lit parades.
April 6 – Chakri Day, commemorating Rama I, founder of the Chakri dynasty.

May 5 – Coronation Day.
May full moon – Wisakha Bucha, Buddha's birthday.
July full moon – Asanaha Bucha, to commemorate the first sermon preached by Buddha.
Aug 12 – Queen's Birthday.
Oct 23 – King Chulalongkorn Day.
Dec 5 – King's Birthday.
Dec 10 – Constitution Day.
Dec 31 – New Year's Eve.

Besides these national public holidays, Thailand has still more festivals which can be national or local, Buddhist or secular, but always joyful and colourful with music and dancing. Some festivals have fixed dates, but mostly they are moveable feasts which follow the lunar calendar.

Ask your rep or at hotel reception for details of any local events: Candle Festivals, Elephant Round-ups, Silk Fairs and River Parades. They are always worth making a special journey.

3.8 Hints and useful addresses

Time Zone: 7 hours ahead of GMT.

Tipping: In all hotels and many restaurants a 10% service charge will be added to the bill, so extra tipping is necessary only for excellent service. It is customary to tip maids and hotel porters (about 30 baht for two or three bags) though not taxi or tuk-tuk drivers.

Electricity: The standard voltage is 220, 50 cycles AC. Plugs are two-pin round or flat type only. Bring a plug adaptor for any gadgets you intend using. Most hotels also have 110-volt outlets for shavers.

Post Offices: are open 8.00-16.00 hrs Mon-Fri, and 8.00-12.00 Sat.

Telephone: To avoid the usual hotel mark-ups on international phone calls, call from a main post office, or buy a Telephone Card which can be used from public card-phones.

Etiquette: The Thais have a reputation for courtesy, gentle behaviour, tolerance and hospitality. Thais do not shake hands (a sweaty habit in a hot climate) but greet you with a palms-together prayer-like gesture called *wâi*. In politeness, make a similar response. You can soon get the habit.

It's 'not done' to lose one's temper, to kiss and cuddle in public, or to wear shoes in a temple. Don't sit cross-legged so that your foot points at someone. It's an insult. There is great respect for the monarchy, and visitors should follow suit. Thais stand throughout their national anthem, which is broadcast daily at 8 a.m. and 6 p.m.

Beachwear: Informality is the rule, but swimwear should be worn only by the pool or on the beach: not in town. Beach nudity is illegal, and is regarded as lacking in respect for Thai traditions of modesty. Topless is frowned upon, though it gets by on tourist beaches.

Health and Safety: The HIV virus linked with Aids is extremely prevalent. Yielding to unprotected temptation is like playing Russian roulette.

Security: As in all major cities, you should avoid carrying large sums of cash and take care to keep hold of your bag to deter pickpockets.

Departure: Individual travellers must pay an airport departure tax of 200 baht.

Speak Thai:
   Sawasdee (khrap/kha) – Hello
   Pen yangai? – How are you
   Sabaay dii – I'm fine
   Plod – Please
   Khob khun – Thank you
   Tao rai? – How much?
   Chai/Mai chai – Yes/no
   Mai pen rai – It doesn't matter

Tourism Authority of Thailand (TAT):
49 Albemarle Street, London W1X 3FE.
Tel: 0171-499-7679. Fax: 0171-629-5519.

TAT offices in USA:
5 World Trade Center, Suite 2449, New York, NY 10048. Tel: (212) 432-0433.
3440 Wilshire Blvd., Suite 1100, Los Angeles, Calif 90010. Tel: (213) 382-2353.
303 East Wacker Drive, Suite 400, Chicago, Il 60601.

Royal Thai Consulate:
29 Queen's Gate, London SW7 5JB.
Tel: 0171-589-0173.
Open: Mon-Fri 9.30-13.00 hrs except on UK or Thai public holidays.

Thomson Agents in Thailand:
Bangkok: Turismo Thai, 511 Sri-Ayutthaya Road.
Tel: 0066 2 247-1466. Fax: 0066 2 246-3993.
Phuket: 5/62-63 Maeluan Road, Amphur Muang, Phuket 83000.
Tel: 0066 76 222404/7. Fax: 0066 76 222409.
Ko Samui: c/o Chaweng Regent Hotel, 155/4 Chaweng Beach, Samui, Suratthani 84140.
Tel: 0066 77 422253. Fax: 422251.
Chiang Mai: 91-93 Mahidol Road, Haiya Muang, Chiang Mai 50000.
Tel: 0066 53 272804. Fax: 271273.
Pattaya Beach: Turismo Thai, 437-15-16 Soi Yodsak, Pattaya, Chonburi 20260.
Tel: 0066 38 361579. Fax: 38 361578.

British Embassy: Wireless Road, Bangkok.
Tel: (02) 253-0191. Open: Mon-Fri 9.30-13.00 hrs.

US Embassy: at 95 Wireless Road, Bangkok.
Tel: (66)-2 252-5040/9.

Chapter Four

Bangkok

4.1 Bangkok stopover

Bangkok became the capital of Siam in 1782, when the ruling King – Chao Phraya Chakri, also known as Rama I – moved his government from Thonburi on the opposite bank of the river.

Founder of the Chakri dynasty which still rules today – today's king is ninth in line – Rama I built two of the city's major sightseeing highlights: the Grand Palace and the enlarged monastery complex of Wat Pho, the Temple of the Reclining Buddha.

Based on the original site of a 16th-century temple, Wat Pho has the longest history of any building in Bangkok. Prior to 1782, the area was just a riverside hamlet, home to a small farming community.

Located on Thailand's principal river, the Chao Phraya, Bangkok is 24 miles upstream from the Gulf of Thailand. As the Siamese capital, Bangkok soon became the country's economic and trading centre, with transport flowing through a network of rivers, streams and canals. Prosperity came from the export of rice from the central alluvial plain, and timber from northern Thailand. Trading was handled by the Chinese community, who actually outnumbered the Thais in prewar years.

Thanks to its intricate canal system, Bangkok became known during the 19th century as the Venice of the East. Then roads were built, to take wheeled traffic. During more recent times, many of the inner-city canals, called *klongs*, have been filled in or paved over – a fact which causes regular flooding during the May to October rains.

In the past fifty years Bangkok has seen rocketing growth as the city became a major-league Asian trading centre, and the home of many regional international organisations.

Population has risen from under a million to the present-day level of over six million, of whom one-fourth are of Chinese descent.

This 20th-century growth has converted an old-time oriental city into a roaring metropolis of traffic-jammed streets dominated by neon signs, glitzy shopping plazas and modern office blocks.

However, you can still find floating markets, the teeming streets of Chinatown, several hundred exquisite jewelled temples and tiny garlanded shrines that tinkle to the music of wind chimes. Lotus-filled sampans glide along waterways that coexist with the bustling modern world.

City of angels

The Thais call their capital *Krung Thep* – City of Angels – which is pushing it a bit. But Bangkok is certainly worth a few days to explore the rich splendours of the Grand Palace, the major temples and the age-old lifestyle of people who live on and beside the klongs.

With enough time to spare, there are still more memorable sights within easy day-trip range.

One basic fact stands out. Bangkok is not an easy city for sightseeing on foot. Only a few tourist sites are grouped closely together. Walking the distances in the heat is not advisable. In steaming Bangkok, most visitors prefer the luxury of air-conditioned transport if available.

As an introduction, a guided city tour is the best solution. This will help you grasp the city's geography, and decide which places to visit again in more detail. Compared with sightseeing costs in Europe, tour prices are modest.

The key sites are featured in a range of different packages, which can also include out-of-town destinations reached by road, river or canal.

On temple and palace tours, ladies should remember to cover their shoulders and knees and no-one should wear shorts. Otherwise, entry may be refused. Inside some buildings, photography is not permitted.

4.2 Palaces, temples and klongs

Grand Palace: A visit normally includes entrance to
the Emerald Buddha Temple which is within the palace grounds. Originally built as a royal residence,
the Palace today is used only for State ceremonies.
(The king today lives in Chitralada Palace, near
Dusit Zoo in northeast Bangkok).

Spread over almost a square kilometre beside the
river, the white-walled complex of the Grand Palace
is packed with an oriental splendour that makes Dis-
neyland seem restrained. Gilded spires, pavilions and
mythological demons combine into a dazzling medley
of colour. Green, golden and orange gables are top-
ped by the ornamental *chofa* – a 'sky tassel' shaped
like a Thai dancer's finger-nail.

Since the foundation by Rama I, later kings have
made many additions. Hence there is some mixture
of architectural styles, with traditional Thai alongside
features of Italian Renaissance or 19th-century Victo-
rian. That exotic mixture came during the reign of
Rama V, when he commissioned a British architect
to build the **Chakri Palace (Maha Prasat)** for Chakri dynasty's centenary. The **Amarin Winitchai Hall**
is used for coronations. At the far end is the
Queen's Elephant Stand, where the royal spouse
could mount directly on the royal elephant's back.

Temple of the Emerald Buddha (Wat Phra Keo):
is the great highlight of the palace complex, and is
certainly the most impressive of all the 400 temples
in Bangkok. The Emerald Buddha, actually made of
green jasper, is claimed to have supernatural powers,
and is newly dressed by the King himself three times
a year at the beginning of each season.

Only 30 inches high, mounted on an orange base,
the Buddha was discovered during the 15th century
in Chiang Rai, north Thailand. This royal chapel
rates as the most sacred monastery in Thailand,
thanks to the supreme image of the legendary Buddha. Rich colour and decoration is everywhere, with
glass-encrusted walls sparkling like jewels.

The palace grounds are open daily 8.30-11.30 and
13.00-15.30 hrs.

Temple of the Reclining Buddha (Wat Pho): also known as Wat Phra Chetupon, is located within walking distance of the Grand Palace, and is open from 8.00 to 17.00 hrs every day. With its 95 pagodas, this is Bangkok's oldest and largest monastery complex, recently restored at considerable cost.

The giant 145-ft statue, 50 feet high, represents Buddha passing into the ultimate state of nirvana. The construction materials are brick, plaster and then the final topping of gold leaf. Of interest are the soles of the mother-of-pearl feet, inlaid with the 108 signs which characterise a Buddha.

The monastery was an early centre of learning, and numerous buildings were dedicated to the teaching of philosophy, literature, astrology, herbal medicine and traditional massage. These activities still continue.

The Marble Temple (Wat Benchamabopit): During the reign of Rama V, white marble was imported from Carrara in Italy to create this masterpiece of Buddhist architecture, the most modern of Bangkok's royal temples. The interior is magnificently decorated, and contains the most beautiful bronze Buddha statue in the country.

Over fifty Buddha images of widely varying style are displayed in a spacious inner courtyard. They are mostly copies of famous Buddhas from other parts of Thailand and neighbouring countries.

Temple of the Golden Buddha (Wat Traimit): Just imagine 5½ tons of solid gold, forming a Buddha ten feet tall. It dates from the 13th century.

The temple is open 9.00-17.00 hrs, entrance free.

Wat Saket and the Golden Mount: If you can face the prospect of climbing 318 steps up an artificial hill, the reward is a splendid panorama over Bangkok as you listen to the evocative sound of wind chimes. The temple itself was built in 1782, and houses a sacred Buddha relic from India, presented to King Rama V by the British government.

The Temple of Dawn (Wat Arun): is Bangkok's best known landmark on the Thonburi bank of the Chao Phraya river. The tallest central spire (called a *prang*) is 282 ft high and is surrounded by four less-er towers, studded with brightly coloured ceramic. This was the royal chapel when Thonburi was the capital. It housed the Emerald Buddha until Rama I moved his government across the river.

The temple is open daily, 8.30-17.00 hrs.

Royal Barges: Close to Wat Arun, on Klong Bang-kok Noi, a huge boathouse shelters the ceremonial Royal Barges. Formerly they doubled as war vessels, but today they are used only once in a while for royal and state occasions. Highly ornate, the barges are interesting for their unique design.

Open 8.30-16.30 hrs.

Vimanmek Teak Palace: Located behind the Na-tional Assembly and opposite Dusit Zoo, the 81-room four-storey mansion built by Rama V in 1900 is claimed as the world's largest building made en-tirely of golden teak. This wood, now rare, is excep-tionally durable, and can last 1,000 years.

The palace (open daily 9.30-16.00 hrs) is a trea-sure house of paintings, china, furniture and personal effects. A one-hour guided tour in English gives a vivid impression of the royal lifestyle.

King Rama V, who reigned from 1868 to 1910, played an effective part in keeping his country free of the colonialism that was sweeping through Asia. He was the first Thai monarch to make state visits to Europe. Rama V was a greatly loved king who had four wives and three consorts who between them gave him 33 sons and 44 daughters.

Understandably, his palace needed large audience and reception areas, and spacious verandahs and ter-races.

National Museum: For anyone who wants to delve deeper into Thailand's artistic heritage, the National Museum is the largest in southeast Asia. The loca-tion is very close to the Grand Palace.

Guided tours in English start at 9.30 hrs.

Jim Thompson's House: A remarkable museum in a traditional Thai house, displaying art treasures, an-tiques, sculptures and artefacts from all over Thai-land and neighbouring countries.

The collection was formed by Jim Thompson, an American architect who first came to Thailand in 1945 as a wartime intelligence officer. He adopted Thailand and soon made his mark by reviving the cottage industry of silk weaving. His efforts put Thai silk back into the world market and certainly contributed to the industry's re-birth.

His disappearance in 1967, during a trip to the Cameron Highlands in Malaysia, has remained an on-going mystery every since. Not the slightest clue has ever been found.

Open Mon-Sat 8.00-17.00 hrs. The entrance fees go to Bangkok's School for the Blind.

Snake Farm: Situated at the Pasteur Institute within Chulalongkorn University, the snakes, including cobras and kraits, are milked of their venom at 11.00 and 14.00 hrs daily, to produce vaccines and serums as antidote for snake bites. Closed weekends.

Klongs and floating markets: Wheeled traffic has long since taken over on the Bangkok side of the river, but the old-time *klongs* – canals – still flourish on the Thonburi side. A trip along the waterways shouldn't be missed, for the incomparable chance of getting a first-hand view of waterside life, little changed across the centuries.

Many tours start from the Oriental Pier on the main river, just by the Oriental Hotel. The usual craft is either a regular motor launch, or a so-called long-tail boat – narrow, and powered by an outboard motor which snarls at high speed, but is tolerable at a more leisured tempo.

A more peaceful alternative is aboard a sedate rice barge which cruises through rural areas.

Some parts of the Chao Phraya River waterfront have a decayed appearance, with decrepit warehouses roofed by rusty sheets of corrugated iron, rotting piles to the jetties, and a total absence of new paint.

But then, rather like a side turning from the broad river, the canal called Klong Dao Khanong leads to an entire network of minor canals.

All along the klongs, one gets close glimpses of family life. Children play at the water's edge, in and out of the water all the time – sometimes hitching a ride by clinging to a passing barge. Some heavily laden barges have their decks awash, in a land where the Plimsoll line is unknown.

On the verandahs of the canalside houses are the household monkeys and dogs; and there are flowers everywhere.

Overall, there is a feeling of rich, abundant fertility, both agricultural and human – all brought to quick ripening by the humid hothouse temperature.

There is wide variety of memorable sights – an occasional temple; tiny side canals, leading through groves of tropical fruit trees; or a sampan with baby swinging peacefully in a hammock.

Depending on the chosen route, you may come to a more exclusive residential section, with solid wooden houses set back amongst the trees.

Some houses are thatched with palm leaves, others with corrugated iron and possibly a TV aerial on top.

The range goes all the way from scenes of squalor to those of great beauty.

On early-morning tours, a popular destination is the Wat Sai Floating Market. There are fruit, vegetable and dried-fish boats, noodle peddlers and floating vendors of coffee or groceries.

Streets around the market are lined with open stalls – grocers, clothiers and dozens of souvenir shops. Tourists often outnumber the locals.

4.3 Trips out of town

Damnoen Saduak Floating Market: is much more 'authentic' than the commercialised klong market of Thonburi. Located in Ratchaburi Province, 65 miles southwest of Bangkok, Damnoen Saduak is the daily scene from dawn till late morning of a great flotilla of sampans, laden with produce. Farm wives barter and sell a huge variety of foodstuffs in this amazing commercial centre.

Nakhon Pathom: En route to or from Damnoen Saduak, a stop can be made at this temple town, to view Phra Pathom Chedi, the world's tallest Buddhist monument, 417 feet high.

Rose Garden: On the return to Bangkok from Damnoen Saduak, many tour groups take a lunch and entertainment break at the 50-acre Rose Garden, 20 miles from the capital.

The lush grounds of this privately owned country resort include an enormous aviary with a fine collection of tropical birds.

Tourist literature leans heavily on glowing descriptions of festival costumes, dances, music, sports and games. On arrival, you usually find that the famous festival was last week. But Rose Garden has the answer. A complete Thai village has been set up with typical farmhouses, barns, windmills, and water-lift devices for irrigation.

Every day at 3 p.m. a complete programme is given of music, dancing, kick boxing, cock fighting, martial arts and sword-fighting. The village culture and sports of every region of Thailand are featured. It would take weeks of travel before a visitor could snap all these subjects in their natural setting.

Every afternoon there's a Buddhist ordination procession, and a girl gets married amid the full ritual of a mock wedding ceremony.

Afterwards, working elephants haul teak-logs and give rides. Altogether a visit to the Rose Garden is well recommended.

Bridge over the River Kwai: Of sombre interest for British and Commonwealth visitors is a ten-hour tour to the River Kwai, where 30,000 Allied war prisoners and 100,000 forced labourers from Thailand, Burma and Malaysia worked on the "Death Railway". The bridge across the river was a key part of the Japanese army project to build a strategic rail link between Thailand and Burma.

Eighty miles northwest of Bangkok, the river flows through the beautiful mountain and jungle-green setting of Kanchanaburi province. The setting is idyllic, but with a single-track bridge as reminder of the appalling loss of life caused by the Japanese.

Ayutthaya and Bang Pa In: Go 50 miles north of Bangkok by road or river to Siam's ancient capital. Luxury boats offer a relaxing view of the Chao Phraya river during a cruise between the ancient and the modern capitals. See section 6.1 of this book.

4.4 Bangkok shopping

For general comments on shopping in Thailand, see section 3.6 in the previous chapter.

Quite apart from Bangkok's choice of department stores, shopping plazas and hotel boutiques, there are several market areas which are fun to visit.

Weekend Market at Chatuchak Park: Crowds gather at this 35-acre market to bring and buy plants, animals, clothes and antiques of every description including many antiques made yesterday. There are also great displays of food. Most colourful is a complete range of pineapple, bananas, and a profusion of exotic fruits like coconuts, rambutans, lychees, betel, mango, mangosteen and rose apples. Faith healers, herbalists, fortune tellers and musicians add extra entertainment.

Chinatown: Here's the main shopping area for Bangkok's estimated 1.5 million people of Chinese descent. Explore the old business centre around Charoen Krung and Yaowarat Road. Especially interesting is Sampeng Lane.

Chinatown bustles with activity day and night. The narrow alleys are crammed with fascinating stalls that sell anything from paper dragons to snake wine and fresh fruit. In gold shops, traditionally painted red and white, the creations are sold by weight at attractive prices.

There's also wide choice of Thai silk, which can be cheaply and quickly made up by local tailors. Amongst the hawkers, look for painters, fortune tellers, flower vendors and the Chinese apothecaries who sell a vast selection of herbs and medicines.

4.5 Entertainment and nightlife

Entertainment in Bangkok ranges from kick boxing to classical dance shows, excellent restaurants and top-grade night-clubs to the wildest of possibilities.

Bangkok's raunchy reputation as a nightlife centre was established during the Vietnam war. At that time, 60,000 American armed forces were based in Thailand. Daily plane-loads flew in from Saigon for a week's 'R & R' – rest and recuperation.

Close to each hotel where GIs were billeted, all facilities grew up: 24-hour-a-day bars, little restaurants, and massage parlours with "pretty girls ready to give good service." Within hours of landing, each GI was fitted out with his R & R girl for the week.

Since the departure of the US military, night-time Bangkok has become part of the tourist industry, with hospitality girls and transvestites who can now talk basic German and Japanese, besides English. A high level of Aids is part of the cost.

Most of the so-called 'girlie bars' are located in the Patpong Road area, between Silom Road and Surawong Road. A street market in fake branded goods and pirate tapes flourishes amid the carnival lighting of discos, go-go bars and massage parlours.

Thai boxing: The unique sport of Thai kick-boxing can be seen on alternate evenings at two stadiums in Bangkok – Lumphini and Ratchadamnoen, usually starting around 6 pm. These offer 'the real thing', as opposed to the brief performances included in shows like those at the Rose Garden mentioned above.

Entrance prices depend on distance from the ringside, ranging from about 100 to 1,000 baht. Each event goes for five rounds at three minutes each. Both boxers appear in the ring with a coloured headband round their foreheads and a tassel or flower at the back. They kneel in ritual prayer – which can last at least two minutes – and then each does a slow half-dance, half shadow-boxing routine.

During the preliminary ritual, the music of two drums and a pipe helps work up enthusiasm. The beat of the music continues relentlessly throughout the subsequent fight.

An occasional bout is fought under Queensberry rules, which make it seem relatively tame: no prayer meeting or drum and pipe music; no feet or knees. Most visitors vote for Thai style every time, so long as they're not in the ring. Some programmes are televised live.

Thai Dinner and Classical Dancing: Leading Thai-style restaurants offer an excellent evening out – a specially prepared Thai meal (usually spiced with moderation) followed by an authentic performance of Thai classical dancing.

Chapter Five

The principal beaches

5.1 Phuket

Reached by direct charter from Gatwick or Manchester by a 530-mile flight from Bangkok, Phuket (pronounced 'Poo-ket') is Thailand's largest island in the Indian Ocean. This holiday pearl of the south is about the size of Singapore, but couldn't be more different.

On Phuket Island the keynote is serenity, fun and relaxation along a string of 13 powder-fine beaches that are scattered in granite coves down the 30-mile west coast.

The island's name derives from a Malay word meaning 'mountain'. Phuket is only a maximum of 13 miles wide, but several peaks top the 1,500-ft level. Every palm-fringed beach offers a beautiful backdrop vista of wooded hills.

When English adventurers explored the region in the 17th century, Phuket was inhabited partly by 'sea gypsies' who lived off shellfish and moved along from one bay to another to give the seafood stocks time to re-establish.

To ensure something like a cash income, some of the semi-nomadic sea people moonlighted as pirates, lurking in sheltered bays while awaiting any prospective booty that came within reach. This enterprise was finally subdued by the English navy during the 19th century.

Meanwhile, the more settled farming communities were principally Muslims of Malaysian origin, while Thais came in somewhat larger numbers as Siamese power spread south from the 13th century.

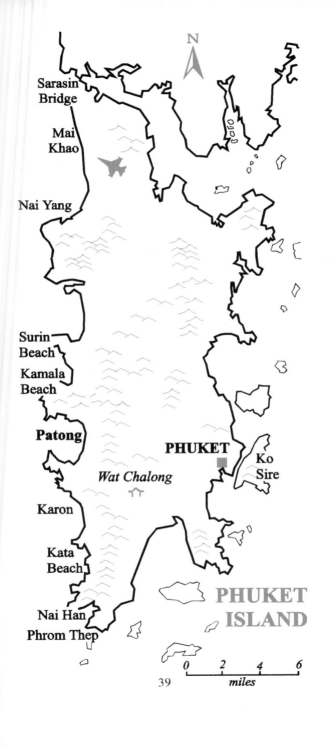

N

Sarasin
Bridge

Mai
Khao

Nai Yang

Surin
Beach

Kamala
Beach

Patong

PHUKET

Ko
Sire

Wat Chalong

Karon

Kata
Beach

Nai Han

Phrom Thep

**PHUKET
ISLAND**

0   2   4   6
miles

An economic boost in the 17th century came from the discovery of rich tin mines which later attracted a flow of Chinese labourers to add more diversity to the ethnic mix. Today's population is 30% Chinese, who mostly have moved up the economic ladder.

Even in the 17th or 18th centuries, Phuket was already a prosperous island, as Europeans competed for trade formerly handled by Arab merchants.

Besides tin, other precious goods were traded from Phuket and neighbouring mainland areas, including ivory, pearls, gem-stones, and ambergris for the perfume industry. From China came demand for the most costly of all foodstuffs: edible birds' nests that gourmets required for soup.

Starting in 1903 an additional source of prosperity was developed: rubber plantations, worked mainly by Muslim smallholders who interplant with luscious pineapple during the seven-year period when the trees are growing to maturity.

Today, Phuket has the highest per capita income of any province in Thailand – over three times the national average. A decline in the value of tin and rubber is balanced by the new industry of tourism.

With ample sources of local investment money, development of the gorgeous west-coast beaches has rocketed in the past twenty years. Phuket is now firmly on the international holiday map.

Patong

The island's most developed beach is Patong, where many leading hotels are located. The 2½-mile crescent is well equipped with every watersport facility, from windsurfers to jet-skis. Powered boats take snorkellers or scuba-divers to off-shore islands.

The turquoise water is warm and inviting. Beach nudity is illegal, but in this cosmopolitan setting the locals now accept that many European women don't have the luggage space for both bits of bikini.

Refreshment service comes round with constant offers of cold beer or fresh pineapple, along with designer T-shirts and other memorabilia. Middle-aged ladies propose an on-the-spot beach massage of the innocent variety; or a beach manicure.

Facing the shoreline, and in The Strip called Soi Bangla which leads up from the beach, is the island's widest choice of shops and night-spots.

Food and nightlife

Lively bars and open-air restaurants offer a full range of Thai and international cuisines, including French, Italian and German. There are pizzas and hamburgers if you want to break away from chilli-happy Thai cuisine.

Best buy is the local seafood, with a particularly good selection of fish restaurants along Soi Bangla. Often you can choose your fish and pay by weight.

Any evening excitement is mainly pitched around the after-dark district off Soi Bangla. Music blares forth from the beer bars, which the Thais call bar-beers. A single male may not stay lonely for long, but there are plenty of holiday couples who just enjoy a drink and the fun of people-watching.

Patong is a good base for exploring the island and for taking all-day cruises to favourite excursion destinations. Scheduled buses, and minibuses called *song-taew*, make the easy 10-mile trip to Phuket Town, the capital city. For more ambitious island touring consider hiring a car or jeep. One day, go south; another day, go north. Be wary of motor-bike rental, which is the biggest single cause of visitor admission to local hospitals.

Although the total island population is relatively small – 180,000 people in an area of 225 sq miles – there is interest in seeing different cultures first-hand: Thai, Malay, sea-gypsy, Chinese. In contrast to the mainland which is 95% Buddhist and 4% Muslim, Phuket is 65% Buddhist and 30% Muslim. There are 28 temples, 29 mosques and 4 churches.

The hilly countryside is full of photo opportunities: waterfalls, lush vegetation, flamboyant trees, village houses on stilts, paddy fields. In palm groves, trained monkeys harvest the coconuts.

Go early morning, and you'll see rubber tappers at work, cutting slantwise into the bark so that milk-white latex oozes into a cup. Later the tappers return to pour the product into trays, to be air-dried into sheets of raw rubber and processed through mangles.

Karon Beach

Three miles south of Patong is the somewhat quieter Karon Beach, with a long stretch of peaceful white sands where the jungle meets the sea. A headland

41

separates the main beach of Karon Yai from Karon Noi (Relax Bay).

A number of resort hotels are spread along the Karon Yai coastline, which is backed by some simple Thai-style eating places and bars for day and night social life. Look for fishermen casting their circular nets into the surf in traditional style. There is good snorkelling around the coral reef.

Kata Beach

Just across a low hill to the south of Karon, the next hideaway is the scenic Kata Beach – another good base for snorkelling around coral reefs en route to Pu Island, which is within reach of a good swimmer.

It's a two-section beach, translating as Big and Little Kata. Shaped like a crescent moon, Big Kata Bay (Ao Kata Yai) is occupied mostly by bungalows and a low-profile Club Med, though the Club doesn't own the beach. The headlands each end of the white sands offer good shelter, to make this one of the Andaman Sea's calmest beaches.

Kata Noi, the smaller bay to the south, is backed by steep green hills.

Touring more beaches

Most of the island's sights can be seen, with occasional detours, along the routes to alternative beaches. Out-of-the-way beaches curve around bays further south, and are highly picturesque with their hillside background. **Nai Han** is home to the sumptuous Phuket Yacht Club which has just about everything except yachts moored to a jetty.

Rated as one of Phuket's prettiest beaches, Nai Han is worth a trip even if Bryan Adams or Mick Jagger are no longer on holiday there. After a swim in the emerald green lagoon, many visitors continue to the nearby **Phrom Thep** cape at the island's southern tip for a spectacular sunset.

Another selection of beaches runs north of Patong, from **Kamala Beach** onwards. Some of the swimming is rough during the monsoon season, with a strong undertow. Take heed of red-flag warnings.

On the most northerly beaches – **Nai Yang** and **Mai Khao**, near the airport – the shoreline shelves steeply. These long sandy stretches are popular with giant leatherback sea turtles who lay eggs ashore during their October-January season. In early March, artificially reared young turtles are helped into the sea as part of a Turtle Release Festival.

At the island's extreme northern tip, the Sarasin Bridge connects Phuket to mainland Asia. Generally, don't waste time on the east coast, where offshore tin dredging has ruined the shoreline.

Phuket Town

The island capital is worth a trip for shopping and to see Thai life in a small-time town of 50,000 with many temples and mosques. The Chinese element is strongest in Phuket Town, which was originally settled about a hundred years ago by Chinese immigrants who came from the Malacca area of Malaysia. Older buildings show a faded Sino-Portuguese style that the settlers brought with them.

In the central market you'll catch the full flavour, variety and smell of Thai food. Shopkeepers are open to bargaining for the standard tourist items. Prices can be lower than Patong's, but less competitive than Bangkok's. Many handicrafts come from other areas of Thailand. Phuket's own specialities include giftware made of seashells, lead-free pewter from local tin, nielloware (silver inlaid with a black alloy) and cultured pearls farmed in Japanese style.

A major event, starting in late-September or October (exact dates depending on the moon), is a ten-day Chinese Vegetarian Festival, based on several Chinese temples in Phuket Town. Daily ceremonies are enlivened with purification ordeals such as firewalking and climbing knife-blade ladders. The local Tourist Office on Phuket Road (phone 212213 or 211036) produces a list of events.

A bridge crosses to the sea gypsy island of **Ko Sire**, where the fishermen's Loy Rua Festival is held just before and after the monsoon.

In fact, virtually every month of the year sees religious or secular festivals around the island, with each ethnic community adding its special colour to the event. Visitors are welcome to participate.

Admission to mosques and temples is open to all who keep to the simple code: wear respectful dress and remove shoes. If you're not visiting the mindblowing temples of Bangkok, **Wat Chalong** is worth seeing for its elaborate architecture.

Off the main road between Phuket Town and Patong is the **Phuket Golf and Country Club**, where non-members are welcome. Opened in 1988, it's a well-planned 18-hole course, 6393 yards, par 72. Phone for reservations: (076) 321-038.

Another 9-hole course is located at Surin Beach.

Exploring other islands

Beautiful boat trips can be arranged from the beach resorts to other islands, which are prolific in this corner of the Andaman Sea. The most popular trips are to Phang Nga Bay and to the Phi Phi Islands.

Phang Nga Bay ('James Bond Island'): A three-hour boat trip goes 46 miles northeast of Phuket to a scenic wonder of limestone cliffs and islands, protected as a National Park. This weirdly beautiful bay is familiar to filmgoers as a setting for the James Bond movie, *The Man with the Golden Gun*.

Green limestone outcrops, honeycombed with caves and aquatic grottoes, soar a precipitous 1,000 feet high from the calm turquoise waters. Few of the islands are inhabited. Boats cruise through a series of canals and low caverns that gleam with stalactites. In one cave there are prehistoric drawings, while another cavern resembles the Blue Grotto of Capri.

A lunch stop can be made at a sea-gypsy fishing village, where the Muslim inhabitants live in houses built completely over the water on wooden stilts.

5.2 Phi Phi Islands

Located a 1½-hour boat trip east of Phuket, the twin islands of Phi Phi Don and Phi Phi Le offer spectacular scenery with coconut groves and jungle foliage.

The main island of Phi Phi Don features pristine white powdery beaches on its southern and eastern shores. The brilliant blue and turquoise waters and a relatively shallow seabed offer superb viewing of coral reefs and teeming marine life. The snorkelling and scuba-diving conditions are ideal. Ton Sai Bay is the main village centre, with bungalows, shops, bars and seafood restaurants.

In contrast, only a 15-minute boat ride away, Phi Phi Le is rocky with towering limestone cliffs. Inside

Main picture, Lake Bratan, Bali
Top Left, Kek Lok Si Temple, Malaysia
Bottom right, Leisurely days in Phuket

Sunset, Kata Beach, Bali

Fishing Boats, Phi Phi

Kek Lok Si Temple, Penang

Floating market, Bangkok

The Grand Palace, Bangkok

Time to smile

To most visitors, these Asian scenes are a highly pleasurable part of the Thai experience. Nobody is in a desperate hurry. There's all the time in the world to gossip, and smile. Even if cash income is very small by western standards, fruit and vegetables grow just as easily as the rice, and it's simple to raise food for a family: chillies and egg-plants, corn and water-melon, cucumber and pumpkins.

Every village home has its own 'spirit house' in a corner of the compound. There are haystacks of rice straw. The more spacious farmhouses are shaded by clumps of trees, and ponds are lively with ducks.

Along the highway, pick-up trucks are crammed with bamboo baskets of fruit and vegetables. Cute village girls ride Japanese motor-bikes and scooters. Gaily-decorated lorries are picked out in vivid green, red and yellow, with Thai pop art around the cabin exterior. Occasionally a few buffalo straggle across the road.

All this, and sightseeing too, in your discovery of Thailand!

Bang Pa In: Thirty miles north of Bangkok is a summer palace built mostly last century during the reign of King Rama V. The houses, pavilions and towers are a gorgeous mixture of Thai, Chinese, Gothic and Renaissance architecture.

Among the colourful buildings is a replica of the Chinese Imperial Court, prefabricated in China and presented to Rama V by the Thai Chinese community.

The lake and gardens make a charming picture-postcard view. In the lake centre is a Thai pavilion renowned for its architectural style. Standing on a green lawn is a unique herd of topiary elephants.

Ayutthaya: Reached by road, rail or river cruiser from Bangkok, the river-island city of Ayutthaya was the capital of Thailand from 1350 to 1767. During that 400-year period, Ayutthaya was rich and powerful, with a line of 33 Siamese kings ruling over Thailand and much of Laos and the Malay peninsula.

Ideally located at the confluence of three rivers, Ayutthaya became a major international trading centre, visited by merchants from China and Japan,

England, Holland, Portugal and France. Travellers declared that Ayutthaya was larger and more splendid than London or Paris.

The sudden end to the glory came in 1767 with a Burmese invasion that sacked and destroyed the city. Today, the magnificent temple ruins, greatly restored, testify to Ayutthaya's former power as one of Asia's principal commercial and cultural centres.

Saraburi: Just north of Saraburi, on the road to Lopburi, is Phra Buddha Pat – the shrine of the Buddha's footprint. It was discovered in mid-16th century when a deer hunter found that a pool of water, shaped like an enlarged human foot, had curative powers.

Lopburi: Dating from the 9th century, this ancient capital of the Khmer people still flourished under Thai rule in the 17th century, when it functioned as a second capital when Ayutthaya was blockaded by the Dutch. An imposing royal palace, partly designed by French architects, survives from that period. It includes the Lopburi National Museum.

Pitsanuloke: Located on the Nan River, this city of 80,000 is famed for the riverside Wat Phra Si which enshrines the bronze Chinarat Buddha. Cast in 1357, it is regarded as Thailand's most precious Buddha image after the Emerald Buddha in the Grand Palace complex of Bangkok.

Sukothai: The first Thai capital from 1238 to 1350, Sukhothai's historic centre has recently been renovated by UNESCO.

Nestling within the original city walls, this rich cultural legacy includes more than 20 major monuments, of which several are dominated by massive stone Buddhas.

The Sukothai era is known to the Thais as 'The Dawn of Happiness', when Buddhism, the arts and the economy flourished.

Si Satchanalai: At this ancient town, dating from the Sukothai period, the temples were decorated with exceptional beauty and originality, much of which still survives in the city ruins.

Lampang: A provincial capital located on the Wang River, 62 miles from Chiang Mai. As a former centre of the teak trade, several Burmese-style temples and other buildings are beautifully constructed of wood. Horse-drawn carriages remain in daily use.

A Thai Elephant Conservation Centre is located 18 miles outside Lampang, where logging training sessions for young elephants are held daily in a forest setting.

6.2 Chiang Mai

Chiang Mai, just over a thousand feet in altitude, is located in a fertile rice-growing plain overlooked by the 5,500 ft Doi Pui mountain peak.

In contrast to the 20th-century capital, Chiang Mai is the much more relaxed market and administrative centre of the North. Serenity is the keynote, though the population is now 160,000.

Well-built teak houses are raised on stilts for good ventilation, with daytime family activities in the cool shade beneath. Luxuriant gardens are filled with roses, hydrangeas and rhododendrons.

Light and airy public buildings are set amid lawns and flowering trees with flamboyant displays of red and pink blossom. The region is also rich in orchid cultivation.

Cheerful tuk-tuk and pedal samlor drivers, some speaking remarkably good English, offer a leisured view of the town and its colourful markets, temples and local craft industries.

Chiang Mai was founded in 1296 by King Mengrai. Several temples are now 700 years old, including **Wat Chiang Man** which was a former residence of the king. From 1556 to 1775 the city was ruled by the Burmese, who built numerous teak temples in Burmese style. Parts of the city wall, forming a square about 700 yards each side and surrounded by a moat, are still intact.

Local colour

Near the markets and at bridge crossings over the Mae Ping River, shutterbugs can get endless colour shots: country women in regional costume, porters with heavily-laden baskets dangling from a yoke across their shoulders, exotic fruits and vegetables for sale beneath large umbrellas, an occasional herd of goats and brightly-decorated country buses.

Early in Chiang Mai history, artisans were encouraged to settle outside the city walls. Chiang Mai today stretches well beyond the original city limits and along both sides of the Mae Ping River. But most of the craft villages still remain in their original locations, while traditions and techniques are quite unchanged from long-ago centuries.

Shopping and sightseeing go together in a popular local industries tour. The Chiang Mai region is home of the principal Thai handicrafts – cotton and silk-weaving on hand looms, manufacture of celadon stoneware, costume-doll making with authentic hill tribe dress, manufacture of paper and silk umbrellas, wood-carving, lacquerware, silver craftsmanship and making of temple bells and Buddhas. Wood carving is of local teak, with elephants, bowls and trays as the favoured subjects.

Visitors are always welcome into the sprawling household compounds, to take photos and watch the simple production lines in operation. It makes an excellent opportunity to see typical Thai interiors and something of family life – even more interesting than another half-dozen temples.

Especially fascinating is the Umbrella Village of **Bor Sarng**, where brightly-coloured umbrellas are made for sale throughout Thailand. Some households specialise in making the frames, others in fitting the paper or silk covers, others in painting the decoration. One can end by visiting half the houses in the village!

Handwoven Thai silk with intricate gold designs is produced both in Chiang Mai and in the neighbouring town of **Lampoon**, 16 miles away. The town's major sightseeing interest is the 12th-century temple of Wat Hariphun'chai. A tall *chedi* or pagoda is crowned by an umbrella of gold.

A few miles further along is **Pasang**, specialising in hand-loom cotton weaving. Pasang is known throughout Thailand as "the town of beautiful girls", owing to their invariable success in beauty contests. The prettiest girls are employed as sales assistants in the stores. Good purchases are sets of hand-woven table mats and runners.

Haggle till midnight

Prices are much cheaper than in Bangkok, to make Chiang Mai an excellent place for shopping. Best buy is a length of Thai silk, unique for its natural look and uneven texture. All these handicrafts are sold in the lively night market, open till midnight, where haggling is necessary.

Another half-day excursion goes up the **Doi Suthep** mountain, offering wide panoramic views of the Chiang Mai area. The hill starts four miles out of town, and the main highlight is the 14th-century temple of **Wat Phrathart**.

Visitors climb 301 steps flanked by brown and green tiles that form a serpent from end to end. Wat Phrathart is a major shrine thronged weekends with colourfully-dressed pilgrims.

Three miles further along is the **King's Palace** – a cool retreat at 4,300-ft altitude. The gardens can be visited on Fridays, weekends and public holidays, except when the royal family is in residence, usually in January.

Seeing elephants at work makes a popular excursion based on travelling out to teak forests where elephant camps are located. A short forest walk is usually necessary to reach the lumber site.

Some tours include a visit to one of the hill-tribe villages – either White Karen or Meo. (See next page for more details about their lifestyle).

In Chiang Mai, the ethnic dances of north Thailand are performed daily, usually as part of a show linked to a traditional dinner called *khantok*. Sticky rice is accompanied with varied curries, local sausage, minced meats and fried rice noodles.

Programmes normally include the famed brass fingernail dance, tribal sword dance, Gingala bird dance, and a Meo hill-tribe dance from the border area near Burma. Some of these dances are rarely performed in Bangkok displays.

6.3 To the Golden Triangle

The far northern corner of Thailand, where the borders of Burma and Laos converge on the Mekong River, is the traditional location for opium-poppy cultivation in the rugged mountain areas.

Hill-tribe cash crops

War-lords were able to cross borders unchallenged, so that great riches were made by those who controlled what became known as the Golden Triangle.

The Thai government has made major efforts to encourage hill-tribe people to abandon their slash-and-burn farming methods in remote forest clearings, by trying to resettle them in lowland areas which permit other cash crops.

The policy has had some limited success, while occasional army forays into the remote hill areas result in destruction of poppy fields. In general, however, illicit production has merely shifted across the frontiers.

A journey to the region must rate among the most scenic of anywhere in Thailand, through the hill-tribe territories.

The tribes originated mostly from China and Tibet some two thousand years ago. For various historical reasons, they moved southwards into Indo-China and Thailand, with the trek into Thailand having accelerated during the present century.

Each of the six main hill tribes has its own distinct culture, religion, language and style of costume. Normally, they live above the 3,000-ft level. They preserve many of their original Tibetan or Chinese traditions, living in extended families.

The road north

On the drive north from Chiang Mai along Highway 107, the initial broad valley looks like a green parkland, through areas that specialise in horse breeding. There are occasional plantations of tea, and of lamgai fruit trees (resembling lychee).

Big irrigation canals water the region, with the network still being extended throughout a wide and fertile area. Two rice crops are grown annually, with virginia-type tobacco as a major cash crop. The green leaf is carted to curing stations, and then packed and exported from Chiang Mai.

Chiang Dao: The scenery grows steadily more dramatic, with thickly forested hillsides reaching close into the Ping River valley, swollen with yellow mud. A side track leads into the Chiang Dao hill tribes reservation.

There are plantations of lychees, pears, pomelo (a fruit somewhat akin to grapefruit), tea and oranges. Near harvest time for the lychees, the fruit is protected in plastic bags against insects, birds and bats.

Fang: This small town features some earth ramparts or fortifications which were erected in 1268 by King Mengrai, the founder of Chiang Mai.

Tha Ton: The departure point on the Kok River for boat trips to Chiang Rai, taking from three to five hours depending on the water level and the type of craft used. Some travellers go by raft.

Here you are very close to the Burmese border. The journey down-river goes past several villages that offer access for trekking parties into hill-tribe territories, staying overnight in bamboo huts. Some treks include elephant transport.

Chiang Rai: The 700 year old city is Thailand's most northerly provincial capital and possesses numerous impressive Buddhist temples. In the heart of the Golden Triangle, the city is overlooked by majestic mountains. Chiang Rai is the principal trekkers' gateway to the surrounding countryside of lush green valleys and hill-tribe villages.

Mae Hong Son: Wedged between Chiang Mai Province and the Burmese border is the Province of Mae Hong Son, with a tiny provincial capital of the same name, population under 7000. Nestling in a valley, this frontier town with its Burmese-style temples thrives on cross-border trade. It is also developing as a tourist centre and starting point for jungle safaris, giving an opportunity to meet hilltribe people – Meo, Karen and Shan.

THAILAND

Langkawi
Islands

KEDAH

Penang

Butterworth

South
China
Sea

PERAK

KELANTAN

TERENGGANU

Taiping

Kuala
Kangsar

Ipoh

Cameron
Highlands

Tapah

Straits
of
Malacca

SELANGOR

PAHANG

KUALA
LUMPUR

NEGERI
SEMBILAN

MALACCA

JOHOR

Malacca

North-South
Expressway

State roads

0 10 20 30 40
miles

MALAYSIA

SINGAPORE

Chapter Seven

Malaysia

7.1 Blending the cultures

Britain's enchantment with Malaysia started in 1786 when Captain Francis Light of the East India Company established the island of Penang as the first British trading outpost in a region controlled at that time by the Dutch. Britain's colonial influence eventually spread throughout this tropical land of rain forests, palm-fringed beaches and clear warm seas.

Independent since 1957, Malaysia's links with Britain remain strong. In September 1998, Malaysia becomes the first Asian country to stage the Commonwealth Games as an integral part of a Year of Sports and Recreation. It's a reminder that Malaysia has some 250 golf courses throughout the country.

Numerous reminders of a British presence still remain, including Penang's historic Fort Cornwallis, and the traditional homes, gardens and plantations of hill stations and retreats in the Cameron Highlands. In Kuala Lumpur, buildings around Independence Square are still colonial in architectural style. English is widely spoken throughout Malaysia.

The mixture of Eastern and Western cultures, history, religion and traditions are among the many attractions that make Malaysia such an exciting and intriguing country to visit. The people are a harmonious racial mix of Malays, Chinese and Indian.

Such diverse cultures produce a mouthwatering variety of cuisine, ranging from hot and spicy to sweet and tangy. There are plenty of five-star hotels with five-star prices, but local restaurants can serve tasty gourmet-style dishes at reasonable cost. It's

possible to enjoy a tasty 3-course meal from a street
hawker's stall for under £1. But alcoholic drinks are
more expensive than in Britain.

About 63% of Malaysia's land area is covered by
forest, including tree plantations. Of that, about 55%
is permanent forest. The country's forest manage-
ment has ensured a network of protected areas which
preserve the natural habitat.

As part of Malaysia's greening programme, the
planting of trees and shrubs in urban areas is
actively encouraged.

7.2 Arrival and orientation

No visa is required by British passport holders, but
the passport should be valid for at least six months
beyond the date of departure.

On disembarking in Penang or Kuala Lumpur,
you should collect your luggage and clear customs.
Visitors bringing in dutiable goods such as video
equipment may have to pay a deposit of up to 50%
for temporary importation, refundable when leaving.
It is advisable to carry your receipt of purchase.

From 1998 Kuala Lumpur has a new International
Airport at Sepang, 38 miles south of the capital but
connected by a new highway and high-speed rail
link. This replaces the airport at Subang which had
reached its capacity. The aim of this largest airport
in Asia is to turn Kuala Lumpur into an airways hub
for south-east Asia.

For Thomson clients to Penang, a rep from the
local agents, Pacific Leisure, will be waiting at the
arrivals exit and will carry a Thomson clipboard.
The agency will organise the transfer to your hotel.

7.3 At your service

Money: The currency unit is the Malaysian Ringgit
– abbreviated as MR or RM or as M$ – which splits
into 100 sen. The approximate exchange rate is RM4
to the pound sterling. Currency notes are issued in
denominations of RM 1,000, 500, 100, 50, 20, 10,
5 and 2. Coins are issued in RM1 and 50, 20, 10, 5
and 1 sen. Credit cards are widely accepted.

Banking hours: 9.30-15.00 hrs Mon-Fri and until 11.30 Sat. Travellers cheques can easily be cashed at local banks and exchange bureaux everywhere.

Transport: Taxi rides are a bargain, especially with petrol costing half what is paid in Britain. Driving is on the left, and the roads are in good condition, often with English-language signs.

In Kuala Lumpur city centre, rush-hour traffic jams are notorious. A new overhead light railway should ease the problem.

7.4 Penang

Malaysia's longest established beach destination is Penang, known as the 'Pearl of the Orient'. The oval-shaped island, 15 miles long and 9 miles wide, lies only two or three miles off the mainland, reached across Penang Bridge or by car-ferry.

On the island's north coast, luxury resort hotels fringe the golden-sand beaches of Tanjung Bunga, Batu Ferringhi and Teluk Bahang. Other beaches are less accessible, though a 46-mile road around the island passes through lush green jungle with access to sandy coves.

There are plantations of cloves, nutmegs and the high-smelling durian fruit. In Malay fishing villages, families live in wooden stilt houses, surrounded by vividly-coloured flowers and bushes, and shaded by coconut trees. En route you can see the production of varied handicrafts and batik textiles.

In the southeast corner of Penang, the **Snake Temple** is home to scores of vipers which are sedated by clouds of incense.

Among the many other natural attractions of Penang, the island is a haven for birdlife, with the official checklist recording over 200 species. These flourish amid the variety of habitats, from beaches and mangroves up to the forested slopes of 2,700-ft **Penang Hill**, which can be reached by road or by funicular railway to the peak for a trainfare of RM3.

Garden-lovers are charmed by the **Botanical Gardens**, located on a bowl-shaped 75-acre site with its own waterfall. Numerous monkeys enliven the shady footpaths among the native tropical plants and trees.

Another show place is the **Butterfly Farm** at Teluk Bahang, where around 120 gorgeous species are reared. The establishment also offers a good range of centipedes, locusts and reptiles.

On an urban circuit, the port of **Georgetown**, site of the original 18th-century trading post, is a fascinating blend of Malaysian, Indian and Chinese cultures.

As a prosperous high-rise business centre, Georgetown teems with traffic. Penang's tallest skyscraper is the 59-storey Komtar building, offering spectacular views from the top.

With Chinese forming more than half of Penang's population, the **Chinatown** district is of the greatest interest, particularly around the waterfront clan piers.

Khoo Clan Ancestral Hall is the most magnificent of the Chinese clan community centres which have continued to play a key role in the culture of Chinese immigrants. When first erected, this hall rivalled the palace of China's emperor, but it was almost immediately burnt down. Rebuilding was on more modest scale, but is still most impressive. Rich carvings and decorated beams pay tribute to the skill of Chinese master craftsmen.

Fort Cornwallis is the site of Francis Light's landing in 1786. There he built a wooden stockade, replaced by stone and concrete in 1804. On the site today is a history gallery, an open-air theatre, a historic Dutch cannon and a handicraft centre.

The Clock Tower was installed in 1897 to mark Queen Victoria's Diamond Jubilee.

Wat Chaymangkalaram is a Buddhist temple in Thai architectural style. Its reclining golden Buddha is said to be the world's third largest, 100 ft long.

Penang Museum and Art Gallery is open daily, and houses historical relics, old photographs and maps; a 19th-century Chinese bridal chamber; paintings, etchings and batik work.

7.5 Langkawi

Just off the Malaysian coast, almost within sight of Thailand, are the 99 islands of the Langkawi group, mostly uninhabited. The only developed island is itself called Langkawi. The attractions are idyllic white-sand beaches, and superb snorkelling along coral reefs teeming with tropical fish that can even be hand-fed.

An island drive can show you lush jungles and waterfalls, rubber plantations, rice fields, fishing villages, a crocodile farm and pine-shaded beaches.

The town of Kuah is a duty-free haven, only a five-minute cab ride from the landing jetty. The main street is lined with a tempting array of shops that offer duty-free international products, besides the locally made batik fabrics and clothing.

7.6 Malacca

Ideal for sightseers and lovers of history and culture, Malacca is a charming 600-year-old town. For centuries Malacca was the greatest trading city of Southeast Asia, handling the rich spice trade, silks, carpets and porcelain. The riches attracted a series of conquerors: Portuguese, Dutch, British and Japanese.

There is much to see from all these imperial occupations, together with the great influx of Chinese traders who intermarried with the Malays. Sailing junks on the Malacca River are a reminder of the city's remarkable maritime history. The port declined as a trading centre through silting of the river and the commercial rise of Singapore. But a major export of rubber continues.

The **Porta de Santiago** gateway is all that remains of the **A Famosa fortress** which the Portuguese built in 1511. It survived several seiges until its final capture by the Dutch in 1641, who restored the damaged fortifications.

When Britain assumed control in 1808, all the massive walls were demolished except for the Porta de Santiago gate, in case the fortress fell into French hands.

The ruined **St Paul's Church** was built by the Portuguese in 1521, and renamed by the Dutch who mainly used the church for its burial ground, and also as an extension to the fortress.

Much more permanent is the **Stadthuys** or Statehouse, built by the Dutch in mid-17th century as a residence for the governor and his officers.

Claimed as the earliest Dutch building in the Orient, the Stadthuys is now the **Museum of Malacca**. Among the exhibits are traditional bridal costumes.

Baba Nyonya Heritage Museum is the ancestral home of a 'Baba Chinese' settler family who merged into the Malay culture through intermarriage. The museum displays this unique fusion of cultures.

Cheng Hoon Teng Temple is Malaysia's oldest Chinese temple, constructed in 1646 by craftsmen from China. Mythical figures on the crossbeams are decorated with painted porcelain and coloured glass.

7.7 Kuala Lumpur

Malaysia's bustling capital, gateway and communication centre offers excellent sightseeing, high quality hotels and some of the best value shopping in Asia, particularly for bargain hunters who can haggle.

Kuala Lumpur's history dates only from 1857, when 87 Chinese tin prospectors established a base and trading post at the confluence of the Klang and Gombak rivers. Large-scale mining in the area led to an expansion of the population, with considerable Chinese immigration.

Within 40 years this commercial centre became capital of the Federated Malay States – chosen for its central location.

The city has seen even greater development in recent decades, mostly high-rise, reflecting Malaysia's booming economy. The most conspicuous sight is the world's tallest building – the Petronas Twin Towers, 1,401 ft high. The Kuala Lumpur Tower with revolving restaurant is only 100 ft lower.

Typically the hosting of the XVI Commonwealth Games in September 1998 has led to spending of £300 million on new sports stadiums and an athletes village to accommodate the event. Another £2m is converting KL into a 'tropical garden' with specially planted trees and flowers along approach roads to sport stadiums.

KL is a city of contrasts, where ultra-modernity mingles with fine examples of gracious colonial architecture, and the temples and mosques of the indigenous Chinese, Malays and Indians who respectively form 50%, 37% and 10% of the population.

Independence Square, otherwise known as Dataran Merdeka, was formerly the sports field of the colonial **Selangor Club**, built in Tudor style. The club still exists, but for a less exclusive membership. On this square, where the Union Jack was lowered on August 31, 1957, Independence Day is celebrated with the Malaysian flag flying from the world's tallest flagpole. Underground is a food, leisure and entertainment complex including indoor golf.

Facing the square is **Sultan Abdul Samad Building**, with its copper domes and fantasy blend of architectural styles. Built in 1897 to house the colonial administration, today it serves the judiciary at one end, and is a handicrafts centre at the other.

In this area of Kuala Lumpur is the **Jame Mosque**, built 1909 in Moorish style at the river junction where the city was founded.

Market venues

The traditional **Chinatown** is centred on Petaling Street, which is partly pedestrianized every evening to form a night market packed with street vendors. Every imaginable product is available, from all the Asian handicrafts to fake brand-name watches and designer perfumes and textiles.

The art-deco **Central Market** has been converted to a centre for Malaysian culture, arts and crafts, with dance and shadow-puppet performances and handicraft demonstrations.

Kuala Lumpur Railway Station, built in 1910, is another example of colonial fantasy architecture with a Moorish flavour. Opposite the Railway Station is the **National Art Gallery**, converted from the former Majestic Hotel. It exhibits contemporary work mainly by Malaysian artists.

Also near the Station is the **National Mosque** (Masjid Negara), completed in 1965 with an 18-pointed star-shaped roof that looks like a partly opened umbrella. The mosque is surrounded by 13 acres of beautiful gardens. Facing the Mosque is the **Islamic Centre**, built in a style that is cubist and Islamic.

A short drive west of the National Mosque are the **Kuala Lumpur Lake Gardens**, comprising 220 acres of pleasure park and botanical gardens laid out around an artificial lake in the 1880s. The **Orchid**

Garden exhibits thousands of varieties, including 800 species from Malaysia alone. The **Butterfly Park** houses over 1230 species; the **Bird Park** features virtually every major species indigenous to Southeast Asia; and there is a **Hibiscus Garden**.

Also within the grounds is the **National Monument**, one of the world's largest bronze sculptures, designed by the artist who created Washington's dramatic Iwo Jima Memorial. It commemorates those who died during a Communist uprising of the 1950s. Alongside is the **ASEAN Sculpture Garden**, displaying prize-winning sculptures from regional artists. Overlooking the Lake Gardens is the modern three-storey **Parliament House** and its adjoining 18-storey tower block.

At the south entrance of the gardens is the stunning **National Museum** in the style of a Malay palace. The facade is decorated with murals that depict colourful historical scenes. Different galleries in the museum have their individual theme: Historical; Cultural; Metalwork and Musical Instruments; Sports; and Natural History.

7.8 Cameron Highlands

There is much interesting countryside along the 140-mile route to the 6,000-ft level of the Cameron Highlands. The road passes oil-palm and rubber plantations to Tapah in the foothills. The winding highway then climbs through jungle country to reach an agricultural area around Ringlet where temperate fruits, salads and vegetables are grown.

Seven miles further along is the main township of Tanah Rata, known for its sparkling air, streams and mountain views.

Along the 38-mile highway from Tapah, a refreshment stop is often made at the majestic Lata Iskandar waterfall. Also worth visiting is a basket-weaving centre and an aborigine settlement.

On terraced slopes of the Cameron Highlands are prime tea and strawberry plantations, which originally supported the colonial life-style with Tudor inns, Devonshire cream teas, rose gardens and golf. The hill-station climate is usually much cooler, often requiring the luxury of an evening log fire in the lounge. Strawberry Park Resort is an international-standard complex with tennis courts and an indoor swimming pool.

For onward touring to Penang, the route returns to Tapah, and then rejoins the North-South Expressway via Ipoh and Kuala Kangsar.

The Perak state capital of **Ipoh** is the centre of Malaysia's open-cast tin mining. But visitors are usually more interested in the **Chinese Cave Temple** of Perak Tong, established in 1926 by a Buddhist monk in a huge limestone cave.

Kuala Kangsar is Perak's royal town, where the Sultan's **Iskandariah Palace** stands on the river bank. Near by is the Perak Royal Museum, containing a wide selection of royal memorabilia. The building, formerly called the **Kenangan Palace**, was constructed without a single nail – and also without architectural drawings!

The **Ubudiah Mosque**, beside the Royal Mausoleum, is rated among the most beautiful in Malaysia.

7.9 Quick facts

Total area: 127,000 sq miles, including Peninsular Malaysia, numerous islands and the northern one-third of the island of Borneo.

Comparative area: about the size of Italy.

Natural resources: tin, bauxite, copper, iron ore, timber, petroleum, natural gas.

Land use: arable land 3%; permanent crops 10%; forest and woodland 63%; other 24%.

Population: 20 million, growth rate 2%.

Life expectancy: 67 years male, 73 years female.

Total fertility rate: 3.3 children born/woman.

Ethnic divisions: Malay and other indigenous 59%, Chinese 32%, Indian 9%.

Religion: Islam is the official religion, but Buddhism and Hinduism are prevalent in the Pensinsula.

Languages: Malay is the official language, but English is widely spoken.

Literacy: 84% (male 89%, female 78%).

Labour force: 7,627,000. Unemployment rate 2.8%.

Government: constitutional monarchy.

Independence: 31 August 1957 (from UK).

Legal system: based on English common law.
The economy: rapid economic development, mixture of private and public sectors. Since 1988 the economy has boomed with an average annual growth rate of 9%, especially due to export of manufactured goods. Industries of the Peninsula are based mainly on rubber, oil, electronics, light manufacture, timber. GDP per capita is around US $ 10,000.

7.10 Hints and useful addresses

Time Zone: 8 hours ahead of GMT.
Security: A very safe country, with low crime rate. But take normal precautions against pickpockets and bag-snatchers in crowded areas.
Tipping: Most hotels and restaurants add a 10% service charge to the bill plus 5% government tax, and extra tipping is not needed except for special service.
Electricity: 220/240 volts AC, 50 Hz. Most hotels also have 110 volt bathroom outlets for shavers.
Post Offices: open 8.00-17.00 hrs Mon-Fri, and until noon on Sat.
Forbidden: Handling drugs carries the death penalty.
Departure: There's an airport departure tax settled direct by some tour operators such as Thomson.

Malaysia Tourism Promotion Board:
Malaysia House, 57 Trafalgar Square,
London WC2N 5DU.
Tel: 0171 930 7932. Fax: O171 930 9015.
Malaysia Tourism Promotion Board – USA:
New York – 595 Madison Ave, Suite 1800, NY 10022. Tel: 212 754 1113/5. Fax: 212 754 1116.
Los Angeles – 818 West 7th St., Suite 804, Los Angeles, CA 90017. Tel: 213 689 9702.

Thomson agents in Malaysia:
Pacific Leisure, 25/26 Angkasa Raya Bldg.,
Jalan Ampang, 50450 **Kuala Lumpur**.
Tel: 03 248 4762. Fax: 03 242 1129.
Pacific Leisure, Unit 227 Penang Plaza,
126 Jalan Burmah, 10050 **Penang**.
Tel: 04 227 0781. Fax: 04 226 9654.

Chapter Eight

Singapore

8.1 Introduction

When Sir Stamford Raffles established a trading post for the East India Company in 1819, today's Singapore was just a fishing village. The rest of the island was covered with jungle and fringed with mangrove swamps. But Raffles saw the potential of the deep natural harbour. Its location at the tip of the Malay Peninsula was ideal to handle southeast Asia's trans-shipment trade which had been a Dutch monopoly.

At the shipping crossroads of Asia, 70 miles north of the equator, Singapore is linked by a causeway to the mainland. The Indonesian islands are to the south, Thailand north, and the Philippines northeast.

Singapore was quickly established in its strategic trading position. Prosperity came from the lucrative traffic in Indian-grown opium, exported to China in exchange for tea. This gateway to the east became even more important when the Suez Canal opened.

Raffles laid down the guidelines for Singapore's growth as a free port, and also launched into urban planning. Separate communities were established for the ethnic groups who flocked to the new boom town: East Beach for European merchants, Kampong Glam for Malays, Serangoon Road for Indians, and Arab Street and Chinatown.

Two statues and a world-famed hotel honour the Raffles name. The colonial-style Raffles Hotel, founded 1887, saw a constant flow of rich and aristocratic guests, writers and film stars. Somerset Maugham spent time here, getting inspiration for his stories of the Orient. The Singapore Sling cocktail was invented at the hotel's Long Bar.

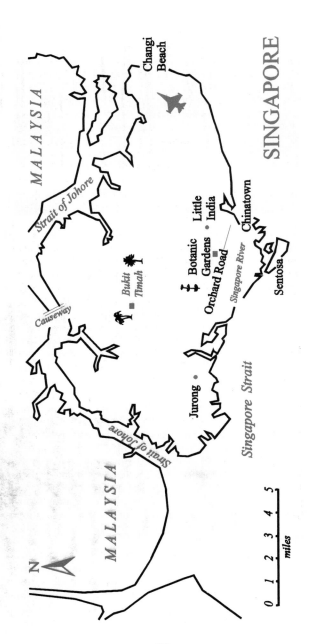

SINGAPORE

MALAYSIA

Changi Beach

Strait of Johore

Causeway

MALAYSIA

Strait of Johore

Bukit Timah

Botanic Gardens
Little India
Orchard Road
Chinatown
Sentosa
Singapore River

Jurong

Singapore Strait

N

0 1 2 3 4 5
miles

Singapore melting-pot

Ethnic variety makes Singapore an interesting destination for its culture, lifestyle and cuisine. The original inhabitants were Malays, who follow Islam and who still, in some areas, live in traditional wooden stilt houses. They represent 15% of the population.

Numerous Chinese arrived from 1821 onwards, mostly as coolies. With intermarriage, they now comprise 76% of Singaporeans. The remainder are Indian, Eurasian and European.

The big shock came during World War II. Fortress Singapore was regarded as impregnable. The garrison commanders figured that their 15-inch guns could easily fend off any seaborne attack, while the dense Malaysian jungle of the mainland would prevent any onslaught from the north.

The Japanese had other ideas. They arrived along jungle tracks by bicycle and forced an Allied surrender within a few days, while all those big guns were pointed the wrong way. On Valentine's Day 1942 the Japanese army cycled into the city and ended over a century of British rule.

Singapore graduated to self-determination in 1959, when Lee Kuan Yew became Prime Minister. Since full independence in 1965, Singapore has seen dynamic economic expansion, to become the world's busiest port in terms of shipping tonnage. At any time there are 700 ships in harbour, and a vessel passes through every six minutes.

Singapore is also the world's third biggest oil refining centre after Houston and Rotterdam, and is a major supplier of electronic components and a leader in shipbuilding.

As a major commercial and financial centre, Singapore has more than 130 banks. World-wide business deals are handled by a high-tech communications network.

Preserving the heritage

Although high-rise buildings dominate the skyline, there are many reminders of the city's history – at Raffles Hotel or Empress Place, in Chinatown or Little India. But it's the future which beckons: a well-planned, efficient garden city with an extremely high standard of living and a developing leisure industry.

Tourism is interwoven with the city's past and future. The industry led the 1980's drive to preserve historic areas of the city, with restoration of the city's landmarks and places of interest. The ethnic communities of Little India, Arab Street, Chinatown and Geylang display the 'Asian Soul' of Singapore. All this, and heavenly shopping too, in a city dedicated to the original Raffles' vision of free trading!

8.2 Arrival and orientation

Singapore's airport on the eastern tip of the island carries a name best known from World War II – Changi, the camp where thousands of Allied prisoners of war were held in gruesome conditions by the Japanese after the surrender of Singapore. Today it's an ultra-modern airport at the centre of Asian and Pacific routes, served by fifty major airlines.

Immigration procedures are swift and efficient. When seeking customs clearance, visitors must declare their cigarettes, cigars or pipe tobacco as these are **not** duty free. But one litre each of wine, spirits and beer is allowed.

After clearing customs, Thomson clients are met by a representative from Pacific World, the local agency for Thomson. The reps wear a burgundy and black uniform and have a Pacific World badge and Thomson clipboard.

For go-it-alone travellers, transport between the airport and downtown is quick and easy by bus or taxi along a 6-lane freeway. The taxi fare from Changi Airport to Orchard Road is about S$15. Bus number 390 to central areas costs S$1.40.

Island features
Singapore is mainly flat with low central hills, the highest being 545-ft Bukit Timah. Large areas of the northeast have been reclaimed, and jungle and swamp cleared. The heart of the city is spread along the island's southern shore. Giving added variety, 57 offshore islets are part of Singapore's territory.

The island is linked to the Malay Peninsula by a causeway carrying a road, railway and waterpipe. The Straits of Johor between the island and the mainland are less than a mile wide.

8.3 At your service

Money: The Singapore dollar (S$ or SGD) divides into 100 cents. Notes are in denominations of S$10,000, 1000, 500, 100, 50, 20, 10, 5 and 1; coins of S$1, and 50 cents, 20, 10, 5 and 1.

The currency is very stable. All exchange is easily handled through official and licensed changers, or at any local bank. Many of these operate branches in major hotels. Reckon around S$2.25 to the pound sterling, or a steady S$1.40 to the US dollar.

Banking hours: 10.00-15.00 hrs Mon-Fri and 09.30-11.30 Sat. Branches of some major banks on Orchard Road are open 09.30-15.00 Sun.

Transport: The Mass Rapid Transit (MRT) system is the fastest and most efficient way to get around. Train and bus fares range from S$0.60 to S$1.50. On buses, have the exact fare ready, as no change is given. One-day or three-day bus Explorer tickets are good value, costing S$5 or S$12.

Singapore has over 10,000 taxis, all metered. Starting fares are S$2.40. Surcharges are made for rush-hour journeys to and from the business centre, and for trips between midnight and 6 a.m. All taxis are easiest to find at a hotel or shopping complex.

Trishaws cater for tourists in Singapore, but are very pricey with no fixed fares. Organised trishaw tours are available.

8.4 Places to visit

To get your bearings, take a half-day orientation tour, showing the principal city highlights, with several stops for exploration on foot. For quick reference, here are the main points of interest that could be short-listed during a 3-day stopover.

Arab Street: A Muslim enclave dominated by the Sultan Mosque, and offering colourful shopping for batiks and other textiles, jewellery, brassware, prayer rugs and exotic perfumes. From City Hall MRT, take bus 171 along North Bridge Road. Possibly combine a visit with Little India below.

SINGAPORE

Botanic Gardens: More than a century of research and care has produced this beautiful 128-acre tropical garden with its manicured palms, a tranquil lake and a spectacular collection of 2,000 species of orchid. Late 19th-century work on rubber plants gave birth to Malaysia's lucrative rubber industry.
MRT to Orchard, then bus 7, 106 or 174.

Bugis Street and Bugis Village: Not the original nightlife rendezvous, bulldozed in 1985, but a sanitized replica on a nearby site with bars, restaurants and a night market. MRT to Bugis.

Bukit Timah Nature Reserve: A 200-acre rainforest reserve, 7 miles from the city centre, embracing Bukit Timah Hill, the highest point of the island. MRT to Newton, then bus. Entrance free.

Changi Prison Museum: A sombre reminder of wartime, when 12,000 prisoners were held by the Japanese in a prison complex built for 600. Photos, sketches and paintings are displayed. Open Mon-Sat 9.30-16.30 hrs, free.
MRT to Tanah Merah, then bus 2.

Chettiar Hindu temple: Among Singapore's most spectacular sights is the gateway to this temple, rebuilt in 1984. But it's just one of many remarkable temples which serve the diverse religions of Singapore. MRT to Dhoby Ghaut, then walk.

Chinatown: Explore this traditional Chinese quarter, wedged in among the high-rise buildings of modern Singapore. The first Chinese migrants settled in Telok Ayer Street where you can see the Thian Hock Keng Temple.

Medicine halls and emporiums line the narrow streets where anything from incense to Mahjong tiles, jade, brocade and dim sum breakfasts are sold. See craftsmen working in shophouses in the Tanjong Pagar conservation area. Great festivities prevail during Chinese New Year.
MRT to Raffles Place or Tanjong Pagar.

Clarke Quay: Shophouses and warehouses near the mouth of the Singapore River have been converted into a 'festival village' of leisure and entertainment. Besides restaurants, hawker stalls, pubs, bars and discos there is an 'adventure ride' which traces Singapore's evolution.
MRT to Raffles Place.

Empress Place Museum: A classical-style court house from 1854, restored to its former glory. It now houses treasures from the Chinese dynasties. Open 9-19 hrs daily, entrance S$6.
MRT to Raffles Place, and walk across the Singapore River.

Geylang Serai: A 19th-century Malay village, best visited for its morning fish and vegetable market. Bus 14 or 16 from Orchard Road.

Haw Par Villa: The former Tiger Balm Gardens is a Chinese mythological theme park, packed with rich colour. Multi-media shows reveal the legends, folklore and culture of China. Open 9.00-18.00 hrs daily, entrance S$16.
MRT to Clementi, then bus number 10; or MRT to Buona Vista, and bus 200.

Jurong Bird Park: A birdlover's paradise with 450 worldwide species. An aviary complex with simulated jungle houses 260 species of southeast Asian birds – one of the world's largest collections. Open 9.00-18.00 hrs daily, entrance S$9.
MRT to Boon Lay, then bus 251, 253 or 255.

Little India: In the Serangoon Road area are the narrow streets, aromatic spices, sari-clad women and Hindu temples that reflect the culture and lifestyle of Singapore's South Indian community. Buses 64, 65, 92 and 111 from Orchard Road. Or combine a visit with Arab Street above.

Mandai Orchid Gardens: A commercial orchid garden next to the zoo. Open 8.30-17.30 hrs daily, entrance S$2. MRT to Yishun, then bus 171; or take bus 171 from Orchard Road.

National Museum and Art Gallery: Established 1887, the museum includes 20 dioramas that follow Singapore's historic growth from fishing village to an ultra-modern city. Lifestyle exhibits focus on the city's heritage.
The art gallery displays works from throughout southeast Asia. Open 9.00-17.30 hrs Tue-Sun, entrance S$1. MRT to Dhoby Gaut, and walk to Stamford Road.

Orchard Road: Singapore's busiest street and main shopping area, the Asian equivalent of New York's Fifth Avenue. Remember that just over 100 years ago it was merely a jungle path.

Padang: The central playing field from colonial times, the home of Singapore Cricket Club, and the 19th-century administrative and social centre. Around the playing field are St. Andrew's gothic-style cathedral built by Indian convict labour; City Hall, where the Japanese surrendered to Lord Mountbatten in 1945; the Supreme Court, dating from 1939; Parliament House, originally a colonial mansion; and Victoria Theatre.

MRT to City Hall, or Bus 390.

Peranakan Place Museum: Displays the lifestyle of the wealthier Chinese who intermarried with local Malays, creating a unique trend in cuisine, architecture and home furnishing.

Open 10.30-15.30 Mon-Fri, entrance S$4. Location is 180 Orchard Road. MRT to Somerset.

Sentosa: In Malay, the word Sentosa means peace and tranquillity. A military base until 1970, it is now Singapore's best known leisure island, reached by cable car from the World Trade Centre to give a thrilling panoramic ride above the harbour. The green 830-acre island offers tropical flora, sandy beaches (imported from Indonesia) and innumerable leisure attractions.

The Asian Village theme park, located next to the ferry terminal, is a 20-acre showcase for Asian lifestyles, food, entertainment, handicrafts and architecture. Elsewhere on Sentosa Island there's a Maritime Museum, a Coralarium that shows the beauty and colour of marine life, a Butterfly Park and a jungle Nature Walk, the Underwater World oceanarium, and a Wax Museum with tableaux that depict the Pioneers of Singapore's history.

Shenton Way: The heart of the financial district, Asia's skyscraper Manhattan and Wall Street.

Tang Dynasty City: A theme park modelled on Chang-An, China's 7th-century Tang Dynasty capital. The market place is crowded with traders and entertainers. A wax museum displays evolution of China's civilisation through 15 imperial dynasties. A pagoda is linked to an underground palace with terracotta warriors, and the added fun of a mock earthquake.

Open daily 9.30-18.30 hrs, entrance S$15. MRT to Lakeside, then shuttle bus.

Gateway to Malaysia: A well-organised one-day tour to Malaysia across the causeway offers a total contrast to the hustle of city life. There's great pleasure from the changing scenery – paddy fields, neat plantations of rubber, pineapple, cocoa and coffee.

Stops are made to see how rubber tappers work, or at an oil palm estate to learn about this fruit and its many by-products. A visit to a Malay village offers a closer look at rural life. A seafood lunch is taken at a fishing village built entirely on stilts, with each house linked to its neighbour by planks.

8.5 Shopping

The slogan is 'Shop till you drop.' Travel out with spare space in your suitcase! Innumerable shops sell duty free goods such as photographic and electronic gear. But do check prices before leaving home to be sure you are getting a bargain, even after any potential payment of UK duty and purchase tax. It's worth re-stocking your film supplies, which are mostly cheaper than back home.

If your purchases from any one store exceed S$500, you can reclaim Singapore's 3% Goods and Services Tax (GST), refunded at the airport.

Most stores open around 10.00 hrs. Some close at 18.30 hrs, while others, especially in the Orchard Road area, stay open until 21.30 hrs.

Department stores have fixed prices which may vary from store to store but can be very good value. Open air market sellers expect you to bargain, and quote an inflated price as starters. Shops which display price tags with a 'recommended price' are also open to haggling.

You can shop in air-conditioned arcades along Orchard Road or in quaint boutiques that sell Chinese silks, brocades and inexpensive clothing. Heaven for ladies; paradise lost for husbands!

8.6 Eating out

Singapore offers a unique chance of sampling a very wide range of Asian cuisine, thanks to the ethnic mixture of Chinese, Malay and Indian.

Blending the cuisines

Special to Singapore is Nonya cuisine – a marriage of Chinese and Malay, developed in early 19th century by Malay wives of Chinese immigrants. The Malay half of the partnership contributed spices and coconut milk to the basic foods of China.

A typical Straits Chinese curry includes ground coriander, chilli, cumin, fennel, turmeric, white pepper, cardamon, cloves, black cumin and cinnamon. These spices are blended with ground-up onion, garlic and ginger, with added salt and sugar.

You can sample Nonya cuisine by exploring around **Peranakan Place**, just off Orchard Road, near Somerset station on the MRT. The delicately painted Straits-Chinese architecture provides the perfect backdrop to Peranakan delights.

Chinese restaurants are everywhere, featuring the cuisines of Canton, Szechuan, Peking and Shanghai. The simplest is just to wander around **Chinatown**.

For Indian cuisine, go to **Little India**, especially in Race Course Road, or in North Bridge Road for Indian Muslim food.

Geylang Serai, the Malay quarter off Geylang Road, offers a rich variety of local Malay food.

In Singapore you can eat from pavement hawker stalls, elegant restaurants or international-type fast-food outlets. You will taste some of Asia's finest cuisines at remarkably low prices. A filling Indian vegetarian set meal at a restaurant on Serangoon Road can cost a mere S$3.

Asian fast food

One of the most exciting and cheapest places to eat is **Newton Circus**. This is the so-called **Hawkers Market** where delicacies of Chinese, Indian, Malay, Indonesian and Western origin are whipped up in a matter of minutes. Among other locations for culinary exploration are the renovated and sanitized **Bugis Street**, and on **Clarke Quay**.

Another place to try is the **Lau Pa Sat Festival Market** in the financial district, where it's a favourite eating place for office workers.

High standards of hygiene are rigidly enforced by the local authorities, to ensure safe eating even from open-air stalls. The tradition, especially in Chinese cuisine, is to use the freshest possible ingredients.

8.7 Singapore by night

The evening can start early with Happy Hour drinks between 17.00 and 20.00 hrs, either half price or two drinks for the price of one.

A sunset cruise aboard a Chinese junk takes the weight off your feet for a restful view of the busy harbour and the scenic southern islands. Admire the waterfront in the setting sun, and see the Singapore skyline assume a different hue as neon lights take over. Some junk cruises feature a sumptuous buffet with tropical fruit.

Another way to enjoy the lights of Singapore is to dine at a rooftop restaurant. Larger hotels offer folk-lore shows and entertainment to accompany a drink or dinner.

Dining out in ethnic restaurants is itself a delight-ful part of Singapore's nightlife. See the previous section for recommended locations, full of character and informal entertainment.

The **Orchard Road** area is the main hub of night-time action. Try to include a visit to the world-famed Long Bar at the Raffles Hotel, and sip their equally famous Singapore Sling cocktail. There are plentiful discos, and nightclubs with all styles of mu-sic, from jazz to bop and worldwide ethnic. Thanks to the Japanese tourist influx, there are numerous karaoke bars.

Tanjong Pagar on the edge of Chinatown has bars, pubs and karaoke lounges galore. There's also lively nightlife at **Boat Quay** and **Clarke Quay** across the Singapore River.

What to wear? Most establishments accept jeans but not shorts, T-shirts and tank tops. In upmarket restaurants and nightspots, a higher standard of dress is expected.

Finally, something different: visit the world's first **Night Safari Park**, open from 19.30 hrs until midnight. In a hundred acres of jungle next to the zoo, you can quietly watch nocturnal animals under subtle artificial lighting.

The animals have ample freedom of movement, giving visitors an insight into the jungle at night, when the creatures are at their most active and natu-ral. Entrance S$15.

8.8 *Quick facts*

Total area: 244 sq miles.

Comparative area: about the size of Middlesex, or 3½ times the size of Washington, DC.

Coastline: 120 miles.

Natural resources: fish, deepwater ports.

Land use: arable land 4%; permanent crops 7%; woodland 5%; other 84%.

Environment: mostly urban and industrialized.

Population: 2.8 million, growth rate 1.2%.

Life expectancy: 73 years male, 79 years female.

Total fertility rate: 1.9 children born/woman.

Ethnic divisions: Chinese 76%, Malay 15%, Indian 6%.

Religion: most Chinese are Buddhist; Malays are Muslim. Minorities include Confucian, Taoist and Christian.

Languages: Mandarin, English, Malay and Tamil. Most Singaporeans are bilingual and use English for business.

Literacy: 88% (male 93%, female 84%).

Press: Locally printed English newspapers are *Business Times*, *Straits Times* and *The Asian Wall Street Journal*.

Labour force: 1,500,000. Financial, business and other services 30%, manufacturing 28%, commerce 22%, construction 9%.

Government: a one-party republic within the Commonwealth.

Independence: 9 August 1965 (from Malaysia).

Legal system: based on English common law.

The economy: Singapore has very strong service, financial, manufacturing and trading sectors. Through the 1970s the economy boomed with an average annual growth rate of 9%, due mainly to strong export demand for Singapore's products.

As one of Asia's economic tigers, Singapore's per capita income is among the highest in Asia, growing since 1980 at over 5% per year.

Singapore is a major oil refining and services centre, and thrives in electronics, oil drilling equipment, rubber processing, ship repair and biotechnology. Inflation is modest, and unemployment negligible.

Agriculture is of minimal importance.

8.9 Hints and useful addresses

Time Zone: 8 hours ahead of GMT.

Security: As in most cities, avoid carrying large sums of cash, and keep firm hold of bags.

Tipping: Most hotels and restaurants add a 10% service charge to the bill plus 4% government tax, and extra tipping is discouraged. Taxi drivers are not tipped. Porters receive a fee of about S$1.

Electricity: 220/240 volts AC, 50 Hz, using UK type 3-pin square plugs.

Post Offices: open 9.00-17.00 hrs Mon-Fri, and until 21.00 hrs on Wed. The Airport and Orchard Point branches are open 8.00-20.00 hrs daily.

Forbidden: Smoking is banned in all air-conditioned public places and indoor restaurants. Lighting up carries a S$175 fine. Chewing gum is illegal. Jaywalkers and litterbugs are fined. Drug abuse carries the heaviest penalties.

Departure: There's an airport departure tax of S$15.00, settled direct by some tour operators.

Singapore Tourist Promotion Board:
1st Floor, Carrington House, 126-130 Regent St., London W1R 5FE. Open 9.00-17.00 hrs Mon-Fri. Tel: 0171 437 0033/4. Fax: 0171 734 2191.

High Commission of Singapore:
9 Wilton Crescent, London SW1X 8SA.
Tel: 0171 235 8315.

Singapore Tourist Promotion Board – USA:
New York – 590 Fifth Ave, 12th Floor, NY 10036. Tel: 212 302 4861. Fax: 212 302 4801.

Chicago – 333 North Michigan Ave, Suite 818, Ill 60601. Tel: 312 220 0099. Fax: 312 220 0020.

Los Angeles – 8484 Wilshire Blvd., Suite 510, Beverly Hills, CA 90211. Tel: 213 852 1901.

Singapore Tourist Promotion Board:
Raffles City Tower 36 04, 250 North Bridge Road, Singapore 0617. Tel: 339 6622. Fax: 339 9423.

Thomson agent in Singapore:
Pacific World Destination Ltd, 26 Horne Road 0502. Tel: 65 291 0288. Fax: 65 291 1634.

British Consulate: Tanglin Rd. Tel: 473 9333.

US Consulate: 30 Hill Street. Tel: 338 0251.

Chapter Nine

Bali

9.1 Jewel of Indonesia

Known as the 'island of the gods', Bali is just one of the 13,677 islands that make up the Indonesian archipelago which stretches from Asia, across the equator, almost to Australia.

But Bali is something special. Its climate, volcanic mountain landscape, rice terraces and especially its gentle people and their intense spiritual life, make the island a traveller's idyll.

As a holiday destination, Bali offers superb white sand beaches, good hotels and all the water sports that are so popular with Australians on holiday.

Festivals and ceremonies take place somewhere on the island every day of the year, with graceful dancing to the evocative music of percussion instruments that comprise a gamelan orchestra.

Although Islam is the main religion of Indonesia as a whole, over 95% of the Balinese practise the Bali-Hindu religion. The fundamentals date from the 15th century, when Muslims invaded Java.

The rulers, priests, scholars and artists fled to Bali, to establish seven kingdoms united by religion. They brought with them centuries of music, culture, art and philosophy, which all flourished.

Today the island has 20,000 temples that range from the Mother Temple at Besakih to tiny village shrines. Joyous celebrations are held in most temples twice a year.

Religion is an integral part of Balinese life. There are rituals that start with ceremonies at birth, and end with a spectacular cremation which frees the soul for its heavenly journey.

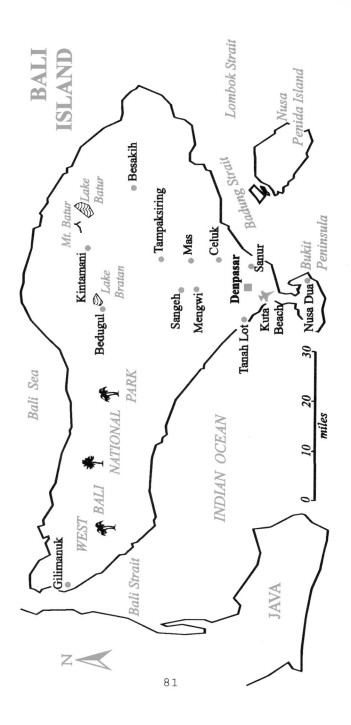

BALI ISLAND

N

Bali Sea

WEST BALI NATIONAL PARK

Gilimanuk

Bali Strait

JAVA

INDIAN OCEAN

Lake Batur

Mt. Batur

Besakih

Kintamani

Lake Bratan

Tampaksiring

Mas

Celuk

Bedugul

Sangeh

Mengwi

Denpasar

Sanur

Tanah Lot

Kuta Beach

Nusa Dua

Bukit Peninsula

Badung Strait

Lombok Strait

Nusa Penida Island

0   10   20   30
miles

Temple etiquette

People wearing white at religious ceremonies are temple guardians, whose requests should be heeded. Also it's polite for visitors to wear a sash on these occasions. Just carry a swathe of brightly coloured material which you can slip round your waist.

Along with the religion goes a tranquil lifestyle that combines cooperation and efficiency, where work, art and leisure seem almost to blend.

Rural cash incomes are small, but nobody goes hungry on ultra-fertile land which yields two or three rice crops a year, with kitchen-garden vegetables and tropical fruit galore. Ducks, pigs and poultry wander free-range around the villages.

Village social life costs time, not money. Music, dance, painting and wood and stone sculpture are normal leisure activities, not merely a pursuit for professionals. It is only in recent years that these exquisite art forms have become a source of income from the tourist industry.

Many of the sights and sounds of Bali will provide memories for a lifetime. Understandably, 85% of all Indonesia's visitors choose Bali, even though this holiday jewel comprises much less than 1% of Indonesia's total land area. Bali is also one of the few islands which has developed an infrastructure for tourism.

9.2 Arrival and orientation

Customs permit duty-free entry of two litres of alcoholic drinks, and 200 cigarettes or other tobacco equivalent. Import and export of more than Rp. 50,000 in local currency is forbidden. Photo equipment should be declared, and must be re-exported.

After going through immigration, Thomson clients are met by a representative from Bil Bali Tours, the local agency. The rep carries a Thomson clip board, and arranges transport to the chosen hotel.

Distances for transfers to Bali's best-developed beaches are quite small: only 6 miles to Sanur, 8 miles to Nusa Dua, or even closer to Kuta. The capital of Bali, Denpasar, is 8 miles north from the airport. Individual travellers can easily find fixed-price taxis.

9.3 At your service

Money: The Indonesian unit of currency is the Rupiah (Rp) which comes in both coins and notes. The exchange rate is around Rp. 4000 to the pound, or Rp. 2400 to the US dollar. Check the current rate on arrival.

Travellers' cheques can be easily exchanged at banks, official money change shops and hotels. The US dollar is the most readily accepted currency. Don't change more money than you need, as only a limited amount of Indonesian currency may be taken out. Keep all exchange receipts, to justify exchange of any surplus on departure.

Banks are open 8.00-14.30 hrs Mon-Fri, and from 8.00-12.00 hrs Sat. Money changers, who often give a better exchange rate, are usually open longer hours.

Credit cards are accepted only by major hotels, restaurants, tourist shops and car-hire agencies.

Transport: Taxis, sometimes air-conditioned, are metered with a set charge per kilometre. Always carry some small-value banknotes, as taxi drivers are often short of change.

Cars and scooters are widely available for hire on production of an international driving permit which is specially endorsed for motorcycles, if required. Generally there's a high risk factor with scooters and motor-bikes, and are certainly not recommended. There's left-hand driving, but local road habits can be somewhat eccentric.

For a more romantic ride try a 'dokar' or jingling horse-drawn cart, but agree a rate in advance. Least expensive are the 'bemo' minibuses which operate along a standard route such as from Sanur to Denpasar. Bicycles can easily be hired.

For more ambitious sightseeing, consider one of the organised tours conducted by a knowledgeable English-speaking guide. You'll see and understand more that way!

An alternative is to hire a car with driver, though his command of English may be somewhat lacking – probably not enough to explain local customs in detail.

9.4 The beach resorts

Beach-holiday Bali is contained within a relatively small area in the southern tip of the island leading down to the Bukit Peninsula. The most famous beaches are at Kuta, Legian and Tuban which have been developed since the 1960s when surfers and backpackers first discovered the region. Beyond that enclave there's all of traditional Bali on your doorstep: a fabulous wealth of sightseeing.

Desa Canggu is a coastal village where the traditional culture still thrives with fishermen, picturesque houses and red-tiled temples in a palm-tree setting. For visitors there is the added attraction of an excellent beach. But swimmers should take care of the tricky currents.

Legian, like several other resorts along this coastline, is a surfers' venue which is a quieter extension of Kuta, only a brief walk away. But Legian itself features a good selection of bars, discos and restaurants, while the shopping for Balinese products has few rivals.

Facing southwest, the beach offers splendid sunsets. Located north of the other resorts, Legian is well placed for sightseeing tours to the interior or up the coast to Tanah Lot Temple.

Kuta is a highly popular tourist resort with a broad sloping beach. It's greatly favoured by young Australians who come for a non-stop beach party. Much of Kuta's long-standing popularity comes from the surfing potential, though currents and the pounding waves make the location less suitable for swimming. Coast guards are on duty throughout the day, but take care to swim only between the flags.

Kuta offers the widest choice of nightlife in Bali, from frenetic bars and discos to performances of traditional music and dance. This former lonely village is now sprawling with the greatest possible range of restaurants, boutiques, tourist shops and accommodation of every price and grade. Yet you'll find age-old rice paddies only a few minutes' bicycle ride inland.

Tuban, a short distance south of Kuta, is quieter in style. It does not have the surfing potential, because an offshore coral reef protects the beach against the waves. Hence this location is more suitable for windsurfing, boating and other watersports. Denpasar, Bali's capital city, can be reached within 20 minutes.

Nusa Dua is located on the eastern side of the Bukit Peninsula, and is home to some of Bali's most luxurious hotels. Unlike the rest of Indonesia, Nusa Dua has been carefully planned, with World Bank help. The development has spotless pavements, tree-lined avenues and landscaped traffic roundabouts.

The resort is famed especially for its magnificent beachfront of clean white sands, clear waters and some of Bali's best scuba-diving and snorkelling along the coral reef. The surf is gentle along the north side of the peninsula, but more boisterous along the south. Transport around Nusa Dua is mainly by taxi.

9.5 Places to visit

Bali beyond the beaches offers a great wealth of sights and experiences. For rich memories, try to see as much of the island as possible. Here's a short-list of highlights which could be covered in two or three half-day or whole-day tours.

Bedugul: A cool and refreshing mountain resort with a local market and botanical gardens. There are lovely views of Lake Bratan, set amid forested hills.

Besakih Temple: High upon the volcanic slopes of 10,300-ft Mt Agung stands the massive sanctuary of Pura Besakih, largest and most holy of Bali's temples. Three main temples, with origins dating from the 10th century, are surrounded by 18 lesser sanctuaries which honour numerous Balinese gods. Festivals are superb. Mt Agung last erupted in 1963.

Celuk: Bali's main silverware centre, with superb craftsmanship. Shops also offer gold jewellery, for which the main centre is Denpasar.

Denpasar: The island's crowded and noisy capital, possibly worth a brief visit for the Bali Art Museum and for a dance performance at the Conservatory of Performing Arts. There's a fixed-price government-run handicraft centre called Sanggraha Kriya Asta, but otherwise shopping is easier at Kuta Beach.

Kintamani: Offers fine views of Mount Batur and its lake.

Mas: South of Ubud, the village of woodcarvers.

Mengwi: The 17th century royal temple of Taman Ayun is one of Bali's most beautiful, well tended and surrounded by a moat.

Mount Batur: A dramatic 5633-ft active volcano with black lava-scarred slopes that overlook the bright blue Batur Lake. The temple of Ulan Danu has been rebuilt since 1926, after the original was destroyed by Batur's last major eruption.

Sangeh: A sacred forest with a 24-acre grove of nutmeg trees, tenanted by very playful monkeys, who are also sacred.

Tampaksiring: One of the earliest centres of Hinduism on Bali. A 1,000-year-old temple is built around a sacred spring. The crystal clear waters are credited with curative powers. Nearby are 11th century royal tombs – Gunung Kawi.

Tanah Lot: Along the west coast, this spectacular temple is perched on a huge offshore rock, reached by a stone causeway. It makes a great picture when outlined against a fiery red sunset.

Ubud: A village art colony and cultural centre, set in beautiful countryside and surrounded by rice fields. Galleries display fine paintings in old and contemporary styles. The Neka Museum displays a wide collection of local art. Regular dance performances are among the best in Bali.

9.6 All the sports

Watersport facilities are well developed, thanks especially to Australian holidaymakers who have been coming to Bali for many years.

Surfing is exciting, particularly at Kuta or Ulu Watu where boards can be hired by the day or hour. Nusa Dua is calmer and better for ordinary ocean swimming.

Explore the coral

Water-skiing, windsurfing, parasailing and scuba diving are easily arranged through your hotel. Outrigger sailing canoes (prahus) can be hired with crew, for trips around the bay.

Snorkelling enthusiasts can enjoy the coral reefs off Nusa Dua and Sanur beaches. Bring your own snorkel, mask and flippers if you have them. The Nusa Dua reef is excellent for scuba-diving.

There are golf courses at Sanur and Nusa Dua – clubs and trolleys available. Most hotels have their own tennis courts and some also have squash. Basic equipment is for hire, but keen players usually bring their own rackets.

9.7 Shopping

Based on a rich art tradition, Bali offers enormous choice of craft products. A full range is available in the tourist shops of Kuta, and a basic selection is offered every five minutes by an ever-friendly stream of beach vendors.

Local paintings are brightly coloured, good quality and excellent value for money. The best choice is available in the artist centre of Ubud.

Other gifts to consider are woodcarvings – often made of ebony – particularly of birds, animals and dancers. The village of Mas, south of Ubud, is the main production centre.

Colourful batik cloth is seen everywhere as part of the daily dress. For the best bargains look around the market or in village stores. Other local crafts include decorative masks, bamboo work, and gold and silver jewellery.

Bargaining is essential and you should be able to reduce starting prices by half in Bali, or by a third in Lombok and Java. If you pay by credit card, many traders expect you to pay an extra 6%, so you will have to bargain harder. In a haggling situation, you can always drive a better deal with hard cash in local currency.

Camera and movie film costs more than in the UK, although processing is cheaper. If you are first passing through other Asian cities, top up your film supplies in Singapore, Hong Kong or Bangkok.

9.8 Eating out

Hotels usually serve a selection of Indonesian, European and Chinese dishes. But it's worth sampling the local cuisine in a genuine Balinese atmosphere. Try these specialities:

Rijsttafel: rice with a mini-banquet of subtle delicacies. A Dutch colonial favourite.

Nasi goreng: fried rice with shrimps, meat and spices.

Babi guling: roast pork.

Opor Ayam: chicken cooked in coconut sauce.

Mango, guava, papaya, rambutan, salak and passion fruit are among the huge range of fruit to try. The adventurous may like to sample durian. Blended squashes are great thirst quenchers.

Imported spirits are available but are costly. The local beer called Bir Bintang, backed by Heineken expertise, gets high marks. If you want something stronger, try arak (a distilled rice brandy) or brem (a sweet rice wine).

Stomach upsets are not uncommon, due to the heat and change of diet. Tap water is not drinkable and it's wise to avoid unwashed fruit or ice cream from street carts. 'Bali Belly' can yield to Lomotil or similar products. Pack some, just in case.

9.9 Nightlife

The liveliest centre is Kuta, where the pace is set by Australians who surf all day and crowd the discos till past midnight. There's also a wide choice of restaurants and bars around Kuta and Sanur.

Some hotels have their own discos and most offer regular evening entertainment. That generally means a shadow puppet play called 'wayang kulit', or some traditional Balinese dancing.

The dance shows could include the spectacular **Kecak** or **Monkey Dance**; perhaps followed by **Sanghyang Dedari**, a trance-like virgin dance; and **Sanghyang Jaran**, a fire dance on a pile of burning coconut husks. The range could feature any other of the main two dozen dance drama routines.

However, far better is to see these performances in their natural festival setting, in the crowded forecourt of a village temple.

9.10 Quick facts about Indonesia

Total area: 740,000 sq miles (Bali 2,147).
Comparative area: 12½ times England & Wales; 3 times Texas (Bali the size of Northamptonshire or Delaware).
Coastline: 34,000 miles.
Terrain: mostly coastal lowlands; larger islands have interior mountains.
Natural resources: crude oil, tin, natural gas, nickel, timber, bauxite, copper, coal, gold, silver.
Population: over 200m (Bali 3m); growth 1.8%.
Life expectancy at birth: 59 years male, 63 years female.
Total fertility rate: 3.0 children born/woman.
Religion: Muslim 87%, Protestant 6%, Roman Catholic 3%, Hindu 2%. (Bali 95% Balinese-Hindu).
Literacy: 77% (male 84%, female 68%).
Government: Republic of Indonesia, capital Jakarta.
Independence: 17 August 1945 from Netherlands; formerly Dutch East Indies.
Suffrage: universal at age 17, and married persons regardless of age.
Economy: A mixed economy with central planning but moving towards deregulation. Indonesia has great natural wealth but remains poor owing to the large and rapidly increasing population. Agriculture, forestry and fishing occupy over half the working population.

Textiles, plywood and plantation crops – rubber and palm oil – are given official encouragement, as a means of creating jobs and earning income from exports. Industry now represents 30% of GDP, with the oil and natural gas sector dominant, generating some 40% of export revenues. Japan is Indonesia's most important trading partner.
Agriculture: Subsistence farming with plantation crops for export – cassava, peanuts, rubber, cocoa, coffee, palm oil and copra. Fruit, vegetables, beef, pork, poultry and eggs are produced for the local market. The staple crop is rice.

9.11 Festivals and public holidays

Literally 20,000 village temples hold a 3-day anniversary celebration every 210 days – the length of the old Java calendar year.

Offerings of fruit, cake and flowers, with ritual prayers and processions, are followed by the music of gamelan orchestras and the performance of dance dramas. It means that ceremonies and festivals are so frequent that you will almost certainly see one, any day that you travel around Bali.

The dances are an art form that is encouraged and practised from early childhood. Among the most popular dances you are likely to see are:

Legong: the heavenly dance of divine nymphs.
Kecak or Monkey Dance: a spectacular circle of up to 150 men chanting and moving as one.
Barong: in which two opposing forces, the benign and the malign, act out their battle.

9.12 Hints and useful addresses

Speak Indonesian: The national language is Bahasa Indonesia, written in Roman script. Over 580 other languages and dialects are spoken locally by the different ethnic groups in the archipelago. Many people in tourist areas also speak English.

Indonesians are particularly polite and respectful and don't even possess a word for foreigner. The nearest translation is 'tamil' or 'guest'. It is courteous to attempt a few phrases and greetings.

Selamat Pagi	– Good morning
Selamat Jalan	– Goodbye
Terima Kasih	– Thank you
Silakan	– Please
Berapa?	– How much?

Electricity: 220/240 volts AC, 50 Hz, mainly with 2-pin round plugs.

Security: Store currency, passport and tickets in safety deposit boxes or hotel safes. Never take valuables to the beach or leave possessions unattended.

Dress: Casual wear is normal, but beachwear or shorts should not be worn when visiting temples. You may need a light sweater or jacket for mountain trips or when attending an evening dance show.

Time Zone: Bali is 8 hours ahead of GMT.

Tipping: At most temples and art museums a donation is normal. Airport porters expect a fee of Rp. 1000 per bag. Leading hotels and restaurants usually add a 10% service charge, otherwise tip 5% to 10% for satisfactory service. Reckon a basic Rp. 1000 tip for cabbies but more for hire-car drivers.

Turtles: Endangered species! Please don't eat any dish containing turtle, or buy turtle products.

Departure: The international airport departure tax is Rp. 17,000. This is settled direct by some tour operators such as Thomson Holidays.

Indonesia Tourist Promotion Office:
3-4 Hanover Street, London W1R 9HH. Tel: 0171 493 0030.
Indonesia Consulate: 38 Grosvenor Square, London W1X 9AD. Tel: 0171 499 7661.
Indonesia Tourist Promotion Office, USA:
3457 Wilshire Blvd., Los Angeles, Calif 90010. Tel: 213 387 2078.

Thomson agent in Bali:
Bil Bali Indonesia Murni Ltd,
Jalan Danau Tamlingan 186, Denpasar.
P O Box 3140, Bali. Tel: (0361) 288464.

British Consulate: Jalan M H Thamrin 75, Jakarta 10310. Tel: (021) 330904.

US Consular agency: 5 Jalan Segara Ayu, Sanur. Tel: (0361) 88478.

Chapter Ten

Hong Kong

10.1 One country, two systems

Many people are curious to see what changes are made by the return to Chinese sovereignty since the historic date of 30 June, 1997. The handover formula of "one country, two systems" declares that the Hong Kong experience will continue for fifty years.

Offering a blend of Asian and Western cultures, Hong Kong keeps a high degree of autonomy as a Special Administrative Region of China.

Under the present rules, UK short-term visitors need no visa (though it's sensible to check again before departure). The Hong Kong dollar stays as the official currency, pegged at 7.80 HK$ to the US dollar, but the Queen's head on coins and notes is replaced by China's national flower, the bauhinia.

English remains an official language alongside Mandarin. The border with China is retained, and incoming numbers of Chinese controlled. With a free trade policy and open economy, Hong Kong continues to flourish as a vibrant international financial centre and a trading gateway to mainland China.

The hotel industry expects a big boom in visitor numbers thanks to opening of the new airport in April 1998. In readiness for the tourist flood, 6,500 more hotel rooms are being built between July 1997 and the year 2,000.

Arrival in Hong Kong is supremely exciting. The view from the aircraft window is one of the world's most thrilling sights. Down below are the islands of Hong Kong, with great variety of vessels that sit like plastic toys on the blue waters – age-old Chinese

fishing junks, rusty tramp steamers, elegant liners, and a hydrofoil trailing its wake on a southward route to Macao.

Travelling to your hotel, you live through a hundred richly coloured movie sets - Chinese people everywhere, noise, Chinese shop signs festooned across the streets, exciting colour everywhere!

For anyone coming straight from Europe, the impact of the Orient is overwhelming. Many visitors immediately go mad on shopping. As a duty-free port, Hong Kong can offer most of the world's manufactured specialities, though at world prices.

Transport is cheap and very efficient. Kowloon to Hong Kong island offers one of the world's great ferry rides, across the busy harbour to the towering skyscrapers that line the Hong Kong waterfront. Prewar there was no building over five storeys.

Sightseeing and enjoying the atmosphere of Hong Kong is best done on foot – wandering around the fantastic streets, seeing Chinese city life first hand.

Another contrast: Hong Kong is much more than just an incredibly overcrowded city. The 'New Territories' bring the former colony's land area to 404 square miles, to give the visitor a chance of seeing rural China in miniature.

Local tour operators feature a 60-mile sightseeing drive. Fascination comes from simple things – seeing rice paddies, duck farms, pigs, water buffalo at work, men and women in coolie hats, and neat vegetable plots. Every mile or two is another village or market town, with all the sights and smells of traditional China. There are duck eggs for sale, mysterious-looking spices, dried fish, cheap clothing, sausages, vegetables, pots and pans.

Old traders with wispy goatee beards sit patiently waiting for customers, while a group gambles with dice in a corner. Take loads of film!

10.2 Arrival and orientation

Until April 1998, visitors land at Kai Tak Airport, skimming the apartment blocks of Kowloon. After going through immigration and customs into the so-called 'Buffer Hall', choose your exit carefully. Walk straight ahead about 20 yards to the Travel

Agent Exits 3 or 4. Thomson clients will be met by a rep from Thomson's local agent, Orient Network.

It's important to ignore Exit 1 which is used mainly by returning local residents and completely independent travellers. So *don't* turn left and down a ramp! Leave money exchange till later, as banks give better rates than the airport moneychangers.

From April 1998 the new airport of Chek Lap Kok takes over. It's the world's second most costly public-works project at £12 billion. The reclaimed island is linked by rail to Kowloon and the financial district, taking 23 minutes for the 21-mile journey. The road alternative is a six-lane highway that includes a suspension bridge almost a mile long.

Orientation
Hong Kong divides historically and geographically into three main areas, comprising a peninsula and 235 islands.

The original 29-sq-mile Hong Kong Island was ceded to Britain in 1842, when the Opium War established Britain's right to export Bengal opium freely into China. The island was barren, but the mile-wide Strait between the island and the mainland formed the ideal deep-water Victoria Harbour. Along the shore today is the Manhattan-style business and financial area called Central.

Across the water, the mainland area of Kowloon was acquired by Britain in 1860. Today the tip of Kowloon – Tsim Sha Tsui – is where most of the tourist and shopping action is located. Much of the present-day waterfront is reclaimed land, built out into Victoria Harbour.

The remaining New Territories, north of Kowloon, and another 230-odd islands were leased from China in 1898 for a 99-year period. The New Territories, about 360 square miles with a 19-mile land border with China, are mainly rural, with hills reaching above 3,000 feet.

10.3 At your service

Money: The local currency is the Hong Kong dollar (HK$), divided into 100 cents, and pegged to the US dollar at HK$7.80. Reckon an exchange rate of around HK$12 to the pound, but check on arrival.

Banks are open 9.00-16.30 hrs Mon-Fri, and until noon Sat. Currency and travellers cheques are easily exchanged at hotels and moneychangers. It's worth shopping around, as rates are flexible.

Check commission charges *before* changing money. They can reach 9%, especially with money-changers who display big signs that say 'No commission on sale'. (That means when you sell HK dollars!).

Transport: Hong Kong's fastest form of transport is the **MTR (Mass Transit Railway)** – an underground system that is efficient, clean, air-conditioned and cheap. But avoid rush hours.

The **Star Ferry** is the world's finest value in transport with bonus sightseeing. Costing HK$2.20 (about 18p) for upper deck 1st class, you ride across the harbour between Kowloon and Hong Kong Island (Tsim Sha Tsui to Central) for an 8-minute journey that will keep your camera clicking non-stop. The green and white ferries shuttle every few minutes.

Double-decker **Trams** trundle along parallel to Hong Kong Island's north shore for another great bargain at HK$1.60 (13p) any distance – exact money needed. Ride them after dark, to view the dazzling neon-lit night scene. Otherwise use the trams for short rides where convenience outweighs the lack of speed.

The funicular **Peak Tram** offers a spectacular route to 1,300-ft Victoria Peak, for a superb panoramic view. The lower terminus is on Cotton Tree Drive, and there's a free shuttle bus from the Star Ferry. Cost is HK$15 single, HK$24 return.

London-type double-decker **buses** are everywhere. They are cheap but can be confusing if you are not sure of your destination and route. Exact change is needed. **Minibuses** which ply set routes and stop anywhere are even more difficult to figure out by short-time visitors.

Taxis are painted red. Taxis won't stop on a yellow line, but are plentiful at cab ranks except during rush hours. The standard of English spoken by the drivers varies greatly, so have your destination written down in English and Chinese. Meters start at HK$14.50 for the first 2 kilometres.

If you cross the harbour tunnel, cabbies charge an extra HK$20 for the return toll. There is no extra charge for air-conditioning. A 10% tip is normal.

On foot: The urban areas are so compact that it is often faster and more enjoyable to walk, especially during peak traffic jams.

Area maps are easily obtained in Hong Kong. Many buildings in Central district are linked by elevated walkways most of the way to Star Ferry and along the quay.

10.4 Places to visit

Hong Kong has the largest number of organised tours in Asia – hardly surprising given the great variety of attractions and sights in the Territory. With everything from architecture to Zen Buddhism, from sports to wildlife, from hiking to horse racing, the range is staggering. The HK Tourist Association has also organised six self-guided walking tours, adding still more sightseeing potential.

The best introduction is a half-day tour of Hong Kong Island, from the business area, Central District, to Victoria Peak for the best view in town and round to the south side of the island.

Another half-day trip skims the surface of urban and industrial Kowloon, combined with a scenic journey through the New Territories.

Hong Kong Island

In the financial Wall Street of Asia called **Central District** are some of the world's tallest buildings. Look, for instance, at the 74-storey Bank of China Building, designed by the world-famed architect I.M. Pei who has modernised the Louvre.

The area is well worth a return visit on foot, to explore the mixture of colonial buildings and the dazzling skyscraper architecture. (MTR to Central or Admiralty Stations).

In great contrast is **Western District**, first settled by the British but which soon became entirely Chinese. Artisans, craftsmen and small shopkeepers follow their traditional trades.

Visit **Western Market** which dates from 1858, the Chinese Merchandise Emporium opposite, and walk through to Ladder Street and Hollywood Road, where the **Man Mo Temple** is dedicated to the Gods of Literature and War.

The tree-covered slopes of **Victoria Peak** are home to Hong Kong's most affluent residents – top civil servants, bankers and executives of trading houses. It's a total contrast to Kowloon's shoe-box tenements, though often the outlook is cloudy.

On southside Hong Kong is **Repulse Bay** with a golden sand beach, fine old buildings, Chinese mansions and luxury apartments.

Another seaside location is residential **Stanley**, best known for its market stalls that sell textiles and designer clothing.

Most memorable is **Aberdeen**, the famous fishing village with a floating community of around 20,000 people living on 2,000 junks. An optional sampan ride gives a close-up view of this age-old lifestyle.

Kowloon

Over in Kowloon, shopping along Nathan Road's 'golden mile' is a huge distraction. But if you want to understand the city better, it's worth visiting the **Museum of History** in Kowloon Park which flanks Nathan Road.

From the Stone Age to the present, the museum gives an insight into the Hong Kong story. The landscaped park also features a Sculpture Walk, an open-air art gallery, and amateur musicians on Sunday afternoons.

Close to the Star Ferry Pier is the **Waterfront Promenade** that offers superb views of Victoria Harbour. The old **Clock Tower** is all that remains of the railway terminus for people who formerly travelled by train from London to Hong Kong.

Close by stands the **Cultural Centre**, a **Museum of Art**, and the white dome-shaped **Space Museum** which faces the prestigious Peninsula Hotel.

At the temple of **Wong Tai Sin**, visitors can have their fortune told after touring the bustling, incense-filled temple. (MTR to Wong Tai Sin).

New Territories

For a breath of countryside, a tour of the New Territories can show you the rolling green hills, market gardens, fish farms and rice fields which lie beyond the bustle of the city. Thanks to improved rail transport since 1980, new towns and industrial areas now flourish – a typical Hong Kong marriage of Chinese tradition and modern technology.

However, the ancient lifestyle has the most interest for the western visitor. Along the west coast from Kowloon, in the Mei Foo district, a popular 3-hour tour destination is **Sung Dynasty Village** – a full size replica of houses, temples and shops from the Sung Dynasty of AD 960 to 1279.

Visitors can sample authentic Chinese food, wine and entertainment of the period. Performers enact a wedding ceremony, and also give Kung Fu displays.

Craftsmen in period costume demonstrate calligraphy, incense manufacture and noodle making. Twentieth-century currency is accepted for purchases.

Just north of Tuen Mun is **Ching Chung Koon**, a Taoist 'Temple of Green Pines' which houses lanterns, a jade seal over 1,000 years old and a remarkable collection of bonsai.

Some tours include a visit to **Kam Tin Walled Village**, dating from the 17th century. Everyone has the same surname – Tang. There are several other single-clan walled villages in the area, with a Tang Ancestral Hall at Yuen Long.

Back towards Kowloon, the Tai Po Road to Shatin passes **Shatin Racecourse**, an ultra-modern facility where the locals gamble heavily.

Close by is the **Temple of 10,000 Buddhas**, where you climb 431 steps to discover 12,800 miniature Buddhas, all different.

If you still have breath, it's worth continuing to the top of the nine-storey pink pagoda for superb panoramic views.

The Outlying Islands

The largest island in the colony is **Lantau**, where people live from fishing, rice-farming and duck-breeding. Visit the Tai O fishing village, built on stilts above the river.

The tranquil monastery of **Po Lin** is home to Asia's largest outdoor bronze Buddha, a benevolent statue perched on a 1700-ft plateau.

Regular ferries also serve **Lamma**, the territory's third largest island, and **Cheung Chau** which has a colourful fishing community of junks and sampans.

10.5 Shopping

Hong Kong ranks high in the world shopping league, with no sales taxes payable. Clothing and Chinese silks are a particularly good buy, with Hong Kong as a major manufacturer of high fashion clothes. Export rejects and overruns are available for bargain prices at factory clothing outlets. Several are located along Granville Road in Kowloon. Street markets offer clothes with fake designer labels.

For electronic and photographic items, check prices in the UK before departure, and calculate what duty and VAT will be payable on your return home. Often, international goods cost only marginally less than elsewhere.

To be confident about a shop's integrity and worldwide guarantees, buy from members of the Hong Kong Tourist Association. At the store entrance, look for the circular Red Junk sticker. The association publishes free shopping guides, listing places like the factory outlets.

Shops open every day including Sunday, except for some department stores. Opening times are usually 10.00-22.00 hrs. Large stores in up-market shopping malls sell at fixed price only.

In street markets and small shops, haggling is necessary, with opening quotes starting high. Check department store prices to figure the maximum to pay.

Where to shop

The Central district of Hong Kong Island has the highest-priced quality stores, such as **The Landmark** shopping mall with big brand name shops.

Pacific Place is a huge complex with an ultra-modern shopping mall, located among three of the most expensive hotels in the territory – Conrad, Marriott and the Island Shangri-La.

Many visitors find it's much more fun to explore Li Yuen Streets East and West, a few blocks west of Star Ferry Pier. These alleys are lined with small shops that sell clothing, shoes, ties and handbags.

In Kowloon, **Nathan Road** is the heart of the shopping area, but there are many other options. Some stores hire people to stand outside and solicit buyers. Westerners can expect a constant sales pitch.

Go to market

For bargains and all the atmosphere of China, try the more colourful market areas. Daily from 10.00-15.30 hrs the junction of Kansu St and Reclamation St becomes a **Jade Market** with rings, brooches and beads spread all over the pavement. (MTR to Jordan, and walk ten minutes north).

The night market on **Temple Street** (also close to Jordan station) is the place for Chinese food, fake brand-name watches and just about everything else from false teeth to palm reading. The **Golden Shopping Centre** on Fuk Wa and Kweilin Street (MTR to Sham Shui Po in north Kowloon) is where you'll find cheap computer hardware, manuals and possibly pirated software, though police action has cut back these copyright violations.

For other electronic goods, visit the crowded **Sai Yeung Choi Street** (MTR to Mong Kok, Bank Centre exit). Only a block or two away is the night market of Tung Choi Street, also called **Ladies Street** for its bargain clothing, cosmetics and music stores. The liveliest time to visit is from 7 to 10 pm. Another block further east is **Fa Yuen Street**, crammed with sport-gear shops.

For handicrafts and other goods made in China, visit the Chinese product emporiums of Kowloon for low fixed prices and no haggling.

10.6 Eating out

With some 20,000 restaurants, Hong Kong certainly offers enough eating choice for a three-day stopover. The most expensive dining is in luxury hotels. Side-street eating places are often better value.

Every style of world cuisine is available. But Hong Kong offers such rich choice of Chinese food, that it seems a wasted opportunity to eat anything else. All the infinite variety of China's regional cuisines is represented, including Hakka, Chiu Chow, Hunan, Peking, Shanghai, Szechuan and Taiwanese. But most restaurants major on Cantonese.

The best introduction to Cantonese dishes is to sample lunchtime *dim sum* any time from 11.00 a.m. to mid-afternoon. Dim sum are bite-sized dumplings of delicately flavoured meat, seafood or vegetables, wrapped in wafer thin dough, then steamed, fried or boiled. Waiters go round with pushcarts, and you pick whatever you fancy. When it's time to pay, they just count the empty saucers. Tea is poured throughout the meal, at no charge.

Maybe you'll want to visit a floating restaurant (the Jumbo Floating Restaurant being the most famous of three floating palaces at Aberdeen). At the other end of the price scale, tasty snacks are available at open-air stalls called dai pai dong.

On the drinks front, Hong Kong boasts the widest variety of teas in the world. San Miguel and Carlsberg beer are both brewed locally. Traditional Chinese wines are served warm. However, their strength and flavour does not always make a good accompaniment to a meal. Tap water is quite safe in Hong Kong, but don't drink a glass of water at a street stall in the New Territories.

10.7 Nightlife

The sight of Hong Kong glowing in a blaze of neon signs is pure magic. For the best views and a sumptuous meal take a harbour cruise at sunset; or visit a roof-top cocktail bar at a leading hotel.

You can watch a performance of Chinese Opera, visit a night market such as Temple Street (mentioned in the shopping section above), go horse racing at Happy Valley on most Wednesday evenings between September and June, or just dance till past midnight in countless discos and clubs.

On Hong Kong Island, Lan Kwai Fong is a narrow street which is the centre of ex-pat nightlife. High-priced bars set amid cobbled hilly streets offer a very Mediterranean-style resort atmosphere.

10.8 Quick facts

Total area: 400 sq miles.
Comparative area: Just over half the size of Surrey, or 6 times Washington, DC.
Land boundary: 19 miles with mainland China.
Coastline: 450 miles.
Population: 5.6 million.

Life expectancy: 77 years male, 84 years female –
ranking third best, worldwide.
Fertility rate: 1.3 children born/woman.
Ethnic divisions: Chinese 98%, others 2%.
Work force: 2,800,000; manufacturing 28%; commerce, restaurants and hotels 28%; other services, finance and insurance 27%; transport and communications 4%.
Overview: Hong Kong is an Asian economic 'tiger' with a flourishing free market yielding an annual 5.5% growth in GDP since 1980. Natural resources are few, and most food and raw materials are imported. With full employment, labour shortage is causing increase in prices and in the cost of living.
Exports: 90% of manufactured goods are exported – mainly clothing and textiles, footwear, electrical goods, watches, clocks and toys.

10.9 Festivals and public holidays

Many of Hong Kong's holidays and seasonal festivals have shifting dates each year, several being dependent on the moon. Check on arrival for any festival which may occur during your stay. The pattern of public holidays is changing with the handover to China. There'll no longer be a holiday for the Queen's Birthday!

Among the many festivals, the great highlight is the 3-day **Chinese New Year** in Jan/Feb.

The **Ching Ming Festival** is a time for families to pay respects to their ancestors, March or April.

The **Cheung Chau Bun Festival** takes place in May on Cheung Chau island, with parades, costumes, and 60-ft towers of buns which are distributed to the crowds.

The **Dragon Boat Festival** is held in May or June, when crews pit their wits and strength against each other in the spectacular setting of Hong Kong Harbour.

The **Hungry Ghost Festival** in Aug/Sep is when underworld spirits come to earth. To appease them, offerings are made.

The **Mid Autumn Festival** in September greets the fullest moon of the year with lanterns on the hilltops, while everyone eats Moon Cakes.

10.10 Hints and useful addresses

Time Zone: 8 hours ahead of GMT.

Security: Very safe, but take care for pickpockets. In emergency, dial 999.

Language: Most people speak Cantonese, with wide use of English for business. English-speaking policemen have a red flash on their shoulder lapels.

Tipping: A service charge is generally included in your bill, and waiters also expect the small change. Otherwise 10% is normal – also for cabbies.

Post Offices: The G.P.O. opens from 8.00-18.00 hrs Mon-Fri, and 8.00-14.00 Sat. Other offices variable.

Electricity: 220 volts AC, 50 Hz. 3-pin round plugs are commonly used, but adaptors are readily available. Many hotels have 110-volt outlets for shavers.

Telephone: Local calls from private phones are free, or HK$1 in coin boxes. To avoid hotel mark-ups on international calls, buy a HK$100 phone card for use from public phones.

Typhoon season: During the June-September heavy-rainfall period, two or three typhoons will affect Hong Kong's weather. Alerts are graded on a scale of 10. Number 3 signals a typhoon heading towards Hong Kong. At number 8 signal, businesses close, public transport stops, and everyone stays indoors.

Departure: Individual travellers must pay an airport departure tax. Check-in counters close 40 minutes prior to flight departure, to discourage late-coming passengers and to improve on-time performance.

Hong Kong Tourist Association:
125 Pall Mall, London SW1Y 5EA. Tel: 0171 930 4775. Open 9.30-17.30 Mon-Fri.

Hong Kong Tourist Association:
11th Floor, Citicorp Centre, 18 Whitfield Road, North Point, Hong Kong. Tel: (852) 807 6543.
HKTA information offices with free brochures etc are located in the basement of Jardine House, at the airport and at Star Ferry Concourse, Kowloon.

Thomson agent in Hong Kong:
Orient Network (Hong Kong), Room 1613, World Finance Centre, Harbour City, Kowloon.
Tel: 00 (852) 2736 7837. Fax: 00 (852) 2376 0329.